Justice and Mercy

Justice and Mercy

Reinhold Niebuhr

Edited by

Ursula M. Niebuhr

1817

Harper & Row, Publishers, San Francisco

Cambridge, Hagerstown, New York, Philadelphia, Washington
London, Mexico City, Saõ Paulo, Singapore, Sydney

FIRST HARPER & ROW PAPERBACK EDITION PUBLISHED 1976.

Designed by Janice Stern

Library of Congress Congress Cataloging in Publication Data

Niebuhr, Reinhold, 1892–1971.
  Justice and mercy.

  1. Sermons, American. 2. Prayers. I. Title.
BV4253.N5 1974   252   73–18704
ISBN 0-06-066175-5

86 87 88 89 MPC 10 9 8 7 6 5 4 3 2 1

God, give us grace to accept with serenity the things that cannot be changed, courage to change the things that should be changed, and the wisdom to distinguish the one from the other.

—1943

Nothing that is worth doing can be achieved in a lifetime; therefore we must be saved by hope. Nothing which is true or beautiful or good makes complete sense in any immediate context of history; therefore we must be saved by faith. Nothing we do, however virtuous, can be accomplished alone. Therefore we are saved by love.

—1951

Contents

PREFACE   *ix*

INTRODUCTION *by Ursula M. Niebuhr*   *1*

1. *Morning and Opening Prayers*   *10*

2. The Providence of God   *14*

3. *Prayers of Praise*   *23*

4. We See Through a Glass Darkly   *29*

5. Law, Conscience, and Grace   *38*

6. *Prayers of Worship and Thanksgiving*   *46*

7. The Wheat and the Tares   *51*

8. Beware of Covetousness   *61*

9. *Intercession*   *70*

10. Be Not Anxious   *76*

11. The Son of Man Must Suffer   *85*

12. *For Nation and Community*   *96*

13. The Burden of Conscience   *105*

14. *For the Community of Faith*   *112*

15. The Hazards and the Difficulties
of the Christian Ministry   *128*

NOTES AND SOURCES   *139*

INDEX OF THEMES OF THE PRAYERS   *141*

Preface

The prayers in this volume have been selected from those Reinhold Niebuhr wrote and used over a span of fifty years. They have been edited according to contemporary liturgical usage. The agreed liturgical texts proposed by the International Consultation on English Texts have provided an example and a standard.

My husband and I had often talked of making this change earlier, when we had planned to publish his prayers. Since his death, the ecumenical connections I have had, further have encouraged and justified this change. Prayers are to be used; so common, i.e., shared, use has been the criterion. Sometimes minor changes of word and style had to be made to correspond to the use of "you" instead of "thou" in the address to God. Otherwise, they are as he wrote them. Many were used in the daily morning services at Union Theological Seminary.

The sermons, however, all come from the later years of his life and are edited from recordings. He never wrote out his sermons. In earlier days he used only a few notes. Later he dispensed even with these. Union Theological Seminary started to record some of his sermons in the fifties. The Memorial Church at Harvard University recorded two sermons in the early sixties, as also did St. George's Church in New York City. These are included in this volume. In this connection, I thank the Reverend Edward Miller, the rector of St. George's, and the Reverend George Buttrick, at that time chaplain at Harvard University, for their kindness in making these recordings available; also the Audio-Visual Department of Union Theological Seminary. Reinhold Niebuhr himself recast some of his earlier sermons into what he called "sermonic essays," in the volumes *Beyond Tragedy* (1937) and *Discerning the Signs of the Times* (1946). In this book, however, the sermons have been edited.

The version of the scriptural text is various. In the prayers, the biblical quotation or "echo" is usually that of the Revised Standard Version or of the New English Bible. In the sermons, the version preserved is whichever one he himself used, as often the logic and force of the argument depend on the particular words quoted. As with many writers, he used a "mixed" text.

My husband and I had hoped to have some of his prayers published long before this. Much of his later work was in the field of social and political ethics. But many of his friends, and he and I as well, wanted to have his prayers and sermons also available to show the religious context and reference of his social concern.

Thanks are due to many who encouraged me in the work of selection and preparation, especially Loretta Evans who first copied out his prayers, and Anne Chase and Margaret Clarke who typed the manuscript, also Mary Misch who gave me much needed help in countless ways.

I am grateful to the Ecumenical Institute for Advanced Studies in Tantur in Jerusalem, where I spent a term in 1973. The community with scholars from different backgrounds and traditions gave me a congenial climate in which to work. James and Frances Scherer, who in student days had known my husband, helped me while they were there, with comment and suggestion. Also, my thanks go to the Sisters of Sion, at whose Ecce Homo Convent on the Via Dolorosa in Jerusalem I stayed while planning this book. Finally, I am grateful to belong to a worshiping community at the Pierce Chapel of Cranwell School in Lenox. My husband's ministry was interdenominational. It would have been his hope that the Ecumenical Institute at Tantur and ecumenical worship such as I have been privileged to share will be the pattern of Christian community and fellowship in the years to come.

U.M.N.

Justice and Mercy

Introduction

By Ursula M. Niebuhr

Reinhold Niebuhr was a preacher and a pastor. These sermons and prayers represent the expression of the two aspects of his ministry.

"I am a preacher and I like to preach, but I don't think many people are influenced by admonition," he said in 1959. "Admonitions to be more loving are on the whole irrelevant. What is relevant are analyses of the human situation that discuss the levels of human possibilities and of sin." A few years earlier, in an address to an entering class of students at Union Theological Seminary, he described the Protestant churches as "too dependent on the sermon. . . . As one who belongs to a quasi-liturgical church, and appreciates the liturgical churches very much, I'd say that the main virtue of the liturgical church is that it isn't so dependent upon the sermon. . . . If a sermon is bad, you can still stand it, because you have the whole drama of faith portrayed in the liturgy." Later, in writing in the late sixties of the great achievement of Catholicism, he described its "sacramental presentation of the mysteries of faith" as "correct" and "more potent than the Protestant sermon, which tends to degenerate into trivial moralizing." He had found, even in the early days of his parish ministry in Detroit, that he had to "put the whole meaning of the sacrament into the prayer."

In 1937 he was urging his fellow Protestant ministers to "take their task as priest seriously." Pleading for "more spiritual reality in the worship service," he wrote: "The priest must know how to express the basic religious aspirations and feelings of a whole congregation. This is a difficult task which requires a high measure of discipline. The discipline is necessary because the temptation is to forget and to

1

neglect the basic and common and perennial religious needs of all men when the prayer is not carefully prepared." In this same article he set forward the relation of social concern "to the basic forms of our faith, and the whole range of religious attitudes," and he then considered the various aspects of prayer in turn.

1. Praise and Thanksgiving

Praise acknowledges God as the author and creator of life. . . . Our thanksgiving ought to include gratitude for what we have, not only through the bounties of nature, but by the working of an intricate system of service and production in modern society. Thus gratitude to God becomes also an expression of our awareness of our mutual dependence and our indebtedness to all who by their faithfulness in their several callings contribute to our necessities.

2. Humility and Contrition

The expression of contrition is a natural consequence of the soul's self-discovery in the sight of God. In worship, we become conscious of our violation of the law and the will of God. We confess that we have done the things we ought not to have done and left undone the things which we ought to have done. Usually this confession of sin is too vague and general. It ought to include contrition for the dishonesties and deceits which we practice in our attitude toward social issues, in which we always mix idealism with self-interest. Naturally, it will express our sense of responsibility for the collective sins which bring society into constant confusion—the violence of nations, the oppression of the weak, our indifference toward the needy, the pride of the powerful, and the envy and jealousy of the frustrated. Human sin expresses itself in every area of human existence, in secret thought as well as overt deeds, in family life and in the relation of the family toward society. The whole range of human sinfulness cannot be touched in each prayer. It is important therefore to deal with a particular area of human wrongdoing from time to time and search the heart in regard to it. But it is also important to express the relation of sins to each other, particularly their common root in the pride of man and the relation of so-called social sins to individual sins.

3. Intercession

Our prayers of intercession express our sense of unity and common responsibility in the sight of God. We will pray for all "sorts and conditions of men." But to discipline the imagination, the sorts and conditions ought to be named and their special needs expressed: the unemployed, the victims of cruelty and oppression, those who live in economic insecurity, the racial minorities who suffer from the arrogance of our race. We might also include in our prayers men of business who stand under particular temptation, that they may regard the services they render as something more than a profit-taking device, and the responsible leaders of government that they may not forget their sacred trust. At certain times we ought also to include the various callings and professions, nurses, teachers, doctors, writers, artisans, housewives, etc., in our intercessions, remembering their particular duties, temptations, and opportunities. Such prayers give specific content to what may otherwise become a meaningless "Lord bless each and every one of us."

4. Aspiration

The prayer "Thy will be done on earth as it is in heaven" must take many forms. We will pray for peace and for a just social order, for the elimination of particular abuses in our common life, but above all we will make it a rededication of our own wills to an obedient love toward God.

In summary, our priestly function must be performed in terms of greater relevance to all the specific problems, personal and social, in which our people stand and in terms of greater contact with the whole biblical and religious tradition of our faith, including the liturgical history of all the Christian churches. We ought, incidentally, not count only upon the resources of our own traditions but use material from all prayer-book sources. Even when we do not use prayers of the past as they have been written, it is well to read them for the sake of acquiring a decent style. If style may seem an inconsequential matter to passionate prophets of the gospel it may be well to remind them that without it they will merely parade their own personalities and prejudices in prayer. A good style is a cloak of anonymity. That cloak is very much needed in our Protestant churches. We preachers constantly border on the abyss of exhibitionism.

"We preachers"—that was how Reinhold Niebuhr regarded himself. He confessed to theological students in 1955 that he was "one who loves preaching more than teaching, a sort of a preacher by instinct—no, I won't say by instinct, but by preference." For more than fifty years, Reinhold Niebuhr followed this vocation—for ten years in his Detroit parish and then increasingly, after his appointment to Union Theological Seminary in 1928, in university and college chapels in different parts of the country.

After his first stroke in 1952 his traveling was restricted, but after two years he resumed his regular visits to Harvard, where he preached for forty-six years, and also, for a shorter period, to Yale and Princeton. Most of his preaching those later years was at the chapel at Union Theological Seminary, also for some years at St. George's Episcopal Church in New York City. Apart from academic pulpits, he preached regularly only at the Germantown Unitarian Church, Christ Church Cathedral in St. Louis (where his great friend, William Scarlett, was

Bishop of Missouri), and the Congregational church in the hill village of Heath, Massachusetts. It was for this church in 1943 that he wrote the well-known "Serenity Prayer," which is quoted as an epigraph to this book. He also preached at the Community Church at Boston, the Sunday Evening Club in Chicago, and in earlier days, the Community Church in New York City, and occasionally for some former student's ordination or installation.

The task of the preacher as Reinhold Niebuhr saw it was to show Christian faith as relevant to life, in both its individual and social dimensions. For him, the Christian faith was "a present fact, and a present truth about life that illumines our existence and gives meaning, relieves us of some of the miseries of guilt in which all men are involved, explains the curious paradox of human freedom and human necessity, of human freedom in spite of the fact that we are living in the necessities of nature." The "effort to establish relevance and the effort to establish applicability," these followed from his basic assumption; so he suggested to his theological students that a good part of their education should be "concerned with validating the foolishness of God as wisdom, but also in relating this wisdom to the wisdom of the world." Appreciative always of the academic congregations to which he preached, he welcomed the climate of our free society, where exchanges of thought and intellectual disciplines took place. "The human soul has so many dimensions as an integral spirit, the pinnacle of which reaches heaven, and asks ultimate questions about the ultimate reasons of existence. . . . But the same human spirit is subject to infinite complexities and maladjustments on different levels," and this means that diversity of disciplines and of understanding our human condition are needed. "For nearly forty years I preached almost every Sunday in various parts of this country. This experience taught me much. 'Making sense' out of the symbols and professions of faith has always been the responsibility of preacher and of teacher."

Reinhold Niebuhr spoke repeatedly and consistently on the second point, the matter of the application of the Christian gospel; for him it was not only the matter of adequate norms in the political and economic order, many and necessary as these are, but to understand the central affirmations of the Christian faith, about the finiteness of man and the sinfulness of man and the holiness of God and the mercy of God in this great drama of history.

Thus transcendent mystery and transcendent love were made plain in the historical measures of justice, in proportionate inter-changes of responsibility and concern between man and man; "the second [commandment] is this, you shall love your neigh-bor as yourself."

Triviality and simple moral absolutes were, to Reinhold Niebuhr, the two begetting sins of the preacher. Often he quoted a remark made by an agnostic friend, who objected to the church "not because of its dogmas but because of its trivialities." This charge impressed him as more valid than any other criticism of religion. By triviality, this friend meant "the disproportionate concern with the minutiae of religious observance, ecclesiastical organizations and sectarian tradi-tion at a time when a whole generation is passing through a world revolution greater than the Communist one. . . . He meant preoccupa-tion with trivial concerns with the world hanging on the rim of disaster." Reinhold Niebuhr continued, "The Church, as every other institution, sinks into triviality when it fails to deal with 'the weightier matters of the law,' . . . which are the law of love and its crown and servant, the law of justice." In this context, he would quote the words of Pope John, "Let love be the motive and justice the instrument."

Calculation of justice—this was the task of responsible citizens and of responsible Christians. In his polemical and journalistic writings, Reinhold Niebuhr often attacked the one-dimensional assumptions of simple moralism; as for example, in *Christianity and Crisis* in 1969, on "The King's Chapel and the King's Court." This article reviewed the semiestablishment of religion of the first Nixon administration with the Sunday service in the East Room of the White House. Reinhold Niebuhr recalled the words of the Prophet Amos, who "was critical of all religion which was not creative in seeking a just social policy—'I hate, I despise your feasts, and I take no delight in solemn assemblies. . . . But let justice roll down like water, and righteousness like an overflowing stream.' " Reinhold Niebuhr wondered whether the clergy who were invited to preach in the White House were not in danger of joining the company of Amaziah, the court prophet of Amos's time, and becoming "high-priests in the cult of complacency and self-sufficiency" which forgets that "all historical reality (including economic, social, and racial injustice) must be subjected 'to the word of the Lord'; i.e., to absolute standards of justice."

His preaching always was based on "the Christian faith, [which] on the one hand asserts the mystery of the Divine, and on the other hand, gives it a specific meaning." This is its "unique character, to have specific meaning given to mystery, rather than to have general principles of meaning, as there are in the great metaphysical systems."

The Bible was the reference, and gave him illustration for his exposition of the faith.

The peculiar genius of the Bible [shows] the ultimate and transcendent character of God [which] challenges man's own conception of piety and goodness—"My thoughts are not your thoughts," etc. The faith of Israel gave the world this vision of a God transcendent over historic process, who also is intimately related to history and to man, and is "as a father who pitieth his children." As transcendence and historic relatedness were bound together in the drama of God and Israel, and of God and man, so also were love and justice held together in the schema of the law. Jesus reiterated this faith of Israel, for it was "the first and great commandment" . . . to "love the Lord your God with all your heart, and with all your soul and with all your mind and with all your strength." The ultimate transcendence was beyond man's exact understanding, for "no man can see God and live," and the glory of God cannot be measured or its mystery plumbed, yet the character of God was made known in "his ways" which were the fulfillments of the law.

. . . The New Testament reiterates this theme in story, parable, and saying with simplicity and immediacy. To his followers, the words and the ministry of Jesus so expressed the message of love (mercy) and justice (righteousness) that he became exemplar and example of "the ways of God."

"For the Christian, the event of Christ—which is not only the person of Christ, not merely the teachings of Christ, but the whole drama of his life, death and resurrection—is the luminous point at which the mystery of the Divine is revealed, and we apprehend this by faith. . . . History is brought to its final pinnacle and the Divine mystery is brought down into history." Yet, also he warned against giving "pat answers to ultimate questions and pat explanations of ultimate mysteries," for all expressions of "religious conviction and affirmation are symbolic. . . . Since we must use symbols to define the reaches of the human spirit beyond definable knowledge, we must realize that these symbols are tangents toward the ultimate, and therefore fruits of the human imagination."

"The Christian Church expresses itself in the framework of prayer," and "corporate prayer is certainly one of the frameworks of faith." So he spoke to his students. In his prayers, the same theme appears as in his sermons; the mystery of creation and of redemption.

The mystery of creation is related to the mystery of God's disclosure in history. . . . The same God who discloses himself as God the Father is the creator. God the Son is the supreme revealer. And . . . this is the same mysterious God whom we encounter as Holy Spirit in all the times of our life when at the ultimate fringes of our consciousness, introspection and meditation are turned into a dialogue. [This dialogue,] . . . the encounter between yourself and God involves . . . repentance and faith of the whole person, . . . [and] always is an encounter which results in dying to live. . . . If we are crucified to the self which is centered around itself, if we are drawn out of ourselves into love of neighbor and love of Christ, we truly live. Life is a perpetual Lent and Easter. It has to be perpetual because we are always falling into new forms of self-centeredness.

The prayers and sermons often echo the words of John Donne, "By thy mercy I have a sense of thy justice," and "I have understood sin by understanding thy law and judgment." "The preacher," Reinhold Niebuhr wrote, "is the mediator of God's judgment and also of his mercy." Too often the preacher lacks charity and humility. "The older I grow in the ministry," he wrote in 1953, "the more I am impressed by good pastors who work with 'those who must be broken before they can be rebuilt; and those who are broken and must be rebuilt.' " Elsewhere, he noted, "in all these pastoral duties, a compassionate heart will show forth the spirit of Christ, and save the Church from triviality."

These sermons and prayers, therefore, are presented to those who share his faith and who find "the human story too grand and too awful to be told without reverence for the mystery and the majesty that transcend all human knowledge. . . . Only humble men who recognize this mystery and majesty are able to face both the beauty and terror of life without exulting over its beauty or becoming crushed by its terror."

1. Morning and Opening Prayers

O God, king eternal, who divided day from night, whose hand stretched out the heavens and commanded all their hosts, who laid the foundations of the deep, who spoke and it was done, who commanded and it stood fast, we worship you who are the creator and source of our life, the preserver of all things that live.

Grant us, our Father, your grace, that, seeing ourselves in the light of your holiness, we may be cleansed of the pride and vainglory which obscures your truth; and knowing that from you no secrets are hid, we may perceive and confront those deceits and disguises by which we deceive ourselves and our fellowmen. So may we worship you in spirit and in truth and in your light, see light.

We thank you, our Father:

For life and love, and for the mystery of existence;

We thank you, our Father.

For all the simple joys of life, and for the world of beauty which surrounds us;

We thank you, our Father.

For good friends who think well of us despite our sins, and for the glimpses of innocence and goodness in a sinful world;

We thank you, our Father.

For all common and uncommon responsibilities which enlarge our souls, and for the pains and sorrows which chasten us so that we be not exalted over much;

We thank you, our Father.

Above all, we thank you for every ministry by which your judgment and mercy is brought home to us;

We thank you, our Father.

O Lord, who has taught us that to gain the whole world and to lose our souls is great folly, grant us the grace so to lose ourselves that we may truly find ourselves anew in the life of grace, and so to forget ourselves that we may be remembered in your kingdom.

We thank you that in your presence all our brothers are the more surely present with us; for knowing them to be included in the breadth of your love, we may feel their claims and needs upon our conscience. We give thanks that you have tied us together in this bundle of life and have ordained that none of us should live to himself alone.

Father Almighty, who are not served by men's hands as though you need anything, but who delights in the worship of a contrite heart, grant us grace in this hour of worship to forswear the pride to which our hearts are prone, to remember that you have made us and not we ourselves, that you are the beginning and the end of our life. Grant us to know the limit of our knowledge that we may seek your wisdom and to know the limit of our power, so that we may glory in your strength which is made perfect in weakness. So may we worship you in humility, and arise to newness of life by fellowship with you.

ᔐᕽᔑ

O Lord, hear our prayers not according to the poverty of our asking, but according to the richness of your grace, so that our lives may conform to those desires which accord with your will.

Where our desires are amiss, may they be overruled by a power greater than ours, and by a mercy more powerful than our sin.

ᔐᕽᔑ

Grant us grace, our Father, to do our work this day as workmen who need not be ashamed. Give us the spirit of diligence and honest inquiry in our quest for the truth, the spirit of charity in all our dealings with our fellows, and the spirit of gaiety, courage, and a quiet mind in facing all tasks and responsibilities.

ᔐᕽᔑ

May we all be given grace to know that our lives are lived over against the perfection of your will. In the light of that knowledge help us to think, speak, and act.

Grant, O Lord, that all who know your law and your will may not be disobedient to the heavenly vision. This we ask by the power of your grace.

ᔐᕽᔑ

O Lord, we pray to you in our perplexity. Let your light so shine in our darkness that our perplexity may not lead us to despair. As perplexity humbles our pride, may we see more clearly what you would have us do.

O Lord, look with favor upon this congregation of your people, gathered together from many parts of the world, called into service and seeking to know your will more perfectly. Instruct us in your work, inspire us by the cloud of witnesses which compass us about, the seers and prophets, the saints and martyrs, of every age, and above all, by your holy spirit in Jesus Christ. Give us grace to learn of each other in the spirit of humility, to pursue our several tasks with diligence, to bear with each other in patience, so that our love may grow in all knowledge and discernment.

2.   The Providence of God

"You have heard that it was said, 'You shall love your neighbor and hate your enemy.' But I say to you, Love your enemies and pray for those who persecute you, so that you may be sons of your Father who is in heaven; for he makes his sun rise on the evil and on the good, and sends rain on the just and on the unjust. For if you love those who love you, what reward have you? Do not even the tax collectors do the same? And if you salute only your brethren, what more are you doing than others? Do not even the Gentiles do the same? You, therefore, must be perfect, as your heavenly Father is perfect."

Matthew 5:43–48, RSV

My text is taken from the New Testament lesson: "But I say to you, Love your enemies and pray for those who persecute you, so that you may be sons of your Father who is in heaven; for he makes his sun rise on the evil and on the good, and sends rain on the just and on the unjust."

This text has been preached upon many times in the memory of all of us. Usually, however, the emphasis has been upon the moral admonition that we should love our enemies, and not much attention has been paid to the justification of the love of the enemy that Jesus gives by reference to the impartial character of God's love. It is on the second theme that I want to speak this morning.

There are many things to say about the first theme, for Jesus is

Union Theological Seminary, New York, February 3, 1952.

suggesting in his Sermon on the Mount that you cannot be moral if you are too strictly moral. The highest morality of forgiveness is, as Berdyaev says, "the morality beyond morality." Nobody who is strictly moral can forgive, because forgiveness is at once the fulfillment of every concept of justice, and its annulment. Jesus justifies this "morality beyond all morality" by saying God is like that. The love of God is an impartial goodness beyond good and evil. The providence of God is an impartial concern for all men without any special privileges in it.

Thus, the structure of meaning for the Christian faith is completed against all the contradictions in history, where there are no simple correlations of reward for good and punishment for evil. God is like nature, says Jesus, like the impartial nature which you could accuse of not being moral at all, because the sun shines upon both the evil and the good, and the rain descends upon the just and the unjust. A nonmoral nature is made into the symbol of the transmoral mercy. Here is a very radical concept, and one of those words of Scripture that we never quite take in. It is a word of Scripture that has particular significance because it is set squarely against most of our religion, inside the Christian Church as well as anywhere else.

When we say that we believe in God, we are inclined to mean that we have found a way to the ultimate source and end of life, and this gives us, against all the chances and changes of life, some special security and some special favor. And if we do not mean that—which is religion on a fairly adolescent and immature level—at least we mean that we have discovered amidst the vast confusions of life what is usually called the moral order, according to which evil is punished and good rewarded, and we could hardly feel that life had any meaning if we were not certain of that.

The Bible is full of this debate between what might be called the instinct of religion and the gospel of Christ. The natural instincts of religion demand that my life be given meaning by a special security

against all of the insecurities of life. If it should seem as if goodness
and evil—punishment for evil and reward for good—were not being
properly correlated in life; then God will guarantee finally that they
will be properly correlated.

Thus, in the Scriptures the words of the Psalms, "A thousand may
fall at your side, ten thousand at your right hand, but it will not come
near you." Or the many intercessory prayers, the intent of which is
"A thousand at your side, ten thousand at your right hand," let it not
come to my loved one. What a natural prayer that is and finally how
impossible! "For in the time of trouble He shall hide me, and he shall
set me upon a rock." In a word, plead my cause, O Lord, against them
that strive with me, fight against them that fight against me.

Examples can be multiplied and it must also be realized how very
natural are these kinds of prayers. Has there ever been a conflict in
the human community where we have not felt we could not fight the
battle were not the Lord on our side? Perhaps, as Abraham Lincoln
said, we did not as frequently ask the question of whether we were on
the Lord's side. These are natural religious instincts, the natural
efforts to close prematurely the great structure of life's meaning.
Much more justified is the other aspect of this sense of special providence—not that God would give me special privileges, special securities against the other man—but that in a very hazardous world where
it is not certain that good will be rewarded and evil punished, at least
God should set that right.

"Blessed is he who considers the poor!" to use another word of the
Psalm, "The Lord delivers him in the day of trouble." Many years
ago, tithing was popular in some of the churches. A member of my
congregation had started tithing as a twelve-year-old boy and had
become a millionaire. He was quite convinced that the millions were
the reward of his tithing.

"Blessed is he who considers the poor! The Lord delivers him in the
day of trouble." I was never much convinced by this millionaire

businessman because of my first pastoral experience when I took the church of my deceased father for six months. The first pastoral problem I had was dealing with an old man whom I greatly respected, who really had the grace of God in him. He had considered the poor to the degree of giving striking miners so much credit at his grocery store that he lost his business. In the seventy-eighth year of his life, he had to face the problem of bankruptcy, and the fact that there was no simple correlation between his goodness and the fortunes of his life.

Both kinds of faith were wrong. First, that if we pray to God fervently enough he will establish some special security for us against the security of the other person. Or secondly, the belief that there are simple moral correlations between the vast processes either of nature or of history and human virtue. The history of our Puritan fathers in New England illustrates how wrong are both of these propositions. There were some very great virtues and graces in their lives. But the doctrine of special providence represents the real defect in our Puritan inheritance. These Puritan forefathers of ours were sure that every rain and every drought was connected with the virtue and vice of their enterprise—that God always had his hand upon them to reward them for their goodness, and to punish them for their evil.

Their belief in special providence was unfortunate, particularly so when a religious community developed in the vast possibilities of America, where inevitably the proofs of God's favor turned out to be greater than the proofs of God's wrath. It may be the reason why we Americans are so self-righteous. It may be also the reason why we still have not come to terms, in an ultimate religious sense, with our responsibilities; with the problems of the special favors that our nation enjoys compared with other nations. But first of all we have to realize that this picture of God's love is not true. The Scriptures also are full of testimony that it is not true. Certainly it is the point of the Book of Job. Job first hopes that God is a God of simple justice, but it is proved to him that this cannot be the case. Then Job protests against the fact that if he does wrong he is convicted as a sinner, but if he does right, he is no better off: "I cannot lift up my head." Ours is a confused kind of world, says Job, in which there is no guarantee that the righteous man will prosper. Is there a God in this kind of world?

These are the protests that run through the Scriptures as they run through life. "My feet had almost stumbled," says the great seventy-third Psalm. "My steps had well nigh slipped . . . when I saw the prosperity of the wicked. . . . Their eyes swell out with fatness, . . . and they say, 'How can God know?' "

"When I saw the prosperity of the wicked"—here is man in history involved in the web of relationships and meanings, but not of simple ones. There must be some moral meaning here. Is there not some punishment of wickedness in life? And I do not mean any of the arbitrary punishment which we inflict by our courts. For life is not completely at variance with itself. There *is* reward for goodness in life, and there *is* punishment for evil, but not absolutely. The same law which punishes the criminal punishes the Savior. And there are three crosses: two for criminals who cannot meet the moral mediocrities of life, and one for the Savior who rises above it. This is life.

Martin Buber, some years ago, made a remark about the special spiritual problems that we face in our world, where we cannot bring to any simple end the structure of moral meaning in which we stand. "When the Nazis ruled," he said, "even when they were at the height of their rule, I knew in my heart that they would fall, that they would be punished."

But now we face a future with greater threats of destruction than during the Nazi period. And this will continue partly because it is a problem that involves all the confusions of modern history against which our own goodness is not adequate. There is no simple moral resolution of the nuclear dilemma. These are the facts of our historic existence; life cannot be correlated easily into simple moral meanings; nor can the Christian faith be validated by proving special acts of providence in your own or somebody else's favor.

I have a certain embarrassment about this issue in the great debate between Christianity and secularism. I am convinced of the Christian faith in the God revealed in Christ and whom Christ says is partially revealed in the impartialities of nature. Yet it seems to me also true that a certain type of secularism has advantages over us on any point where, to quote William James, Christianity becomes "an effort to lobby in the courts of the Almighty for special favors."

Against this lobbying for special favors, one must admit that there is an element of nobility either in modern or ancient Stoicism. Marcus Aurelius said: "If so be the gods deliberated in particular on those things that should happen to me, I must stand to their deliberation, but if so be that they have not deliberated for me in particular, certainly they have on the whole and in general deliberated on those things which happen to me. In consequence and coherence of this general deliberation, I am bound to embrace and to accept them." There is a certain nobility in Stoic courage. It has no sense of an ultimate relationship to God as a final expression of the Christian faith, but as far as it goes, is it not true?

Modern man, under the influence of natural science, sees the problem more critically than it was seen before. We see that nature, whatever may be God's ultimate sovereignty over it, moves by its own laws. Even so good a theologian as the late William Temple did not understand this. He tried to solve it by saying the laws of nature are merely God's habitual way of doing things. If he does not want to act in the habitual way, he will choose another way. Surely this is too voluntaristic a conception of how the forces of nature work.

An analogous proposition would be that my heart beats in a habitual way, but if I choose, I could have it do something else. No, my heart has its own automatic processes as do the forces of nature. Many in our modern world have come to despair about this vast realm of seeming meaninglessness.

Though we have some sympathy from a modern scientific culture which says such special providence is not true, what concerns us more as Christians is the protest of Jesus against the underlying assumptions. It is not true that God gives special favors, and it is not true that there are simple moral meanings in the processes of history. We cannot speak simply of a moral order which if defied, would destroy us. Though Jesus is concerned about the whole dimension of the gospel, it is not so much whether these things are true or not upon their own levels, but whether they would be right. God's love would not be right if it were this kind of a love. This is the point that Christ makes in the Sermon on the Mount, that God's love would not be right. The Christian faith believes that within and beyond the tragedies and the contradictions of history we have laid hold upon a loving heart, the proof of whose love is first impartiality toward all of his children, and secondly a mercy which transcends good and evil.

How shall we appropriate this insistence of Christ in our life? All of us, including some who are not conventionally religious, have a desire for an ultimate security. Even people who are not conventionally religious often pray in the hour of crisis. In that sense, all men are religious. Yet under the discipline of the gospel, we should bring each one of these prayers under scrutiny.

This does not change radically the problem of intercessory prayer. Perhaps we have to consider life in three different dimensions. First, there is the vast dimension of nature where we cannot expect that God will put up a special umbrella for us against this or that possible disaster. In the realm of nature, we face the problem of natural evil. Jesus was asked, "Master, who sinned, this man or his parents, that he was born blind?" Jesus' answer repudiated the idea of special providence: "It was not that this man sinned or his parents have sinned but that the works of God might be made manifest in him." There is no meaning to this blindness except the ultimate possible meaning of how the blindness might become a source of grace. It is a most terrible thing to correlate natural evil immediately to any moral and spiritual meaning, and yet it is a wonderful thing to correlate it ultimately. Likewise Jesus replied, when asked about those killed by the fall of the tower in Siloam, "Were they worse offenders than all the others who dwell in Jerusalem? I tell you, no!" Do not try to relate natural catastrophes to moral meanings. Do not ask the question whether people killed in an earthquake are more guilty, more sinful, than others. "I tell you, no!" Ask the question, rather, what ultimate use, what final point for the grace of God is there in this calamity? But do not correlate it in such a way that it ceases to be a calamity, for this belongs to the realm of nature.

In the realm of history we have another problem, of course, because history is a realm of human freedom and human agency, and if it did not have any moral meaning at all, it would be intolerable. If there were not some reward for goodness, life would be absolutely askew. If there were no likelihood that forgiveness would produce the spirit of forgiveness, and mutuality the spirit of mutuality and reciprocity, it would be hard to love and trust each other. Yet in the processes of history these things are not simply correlated. The suffering of the innocent is one of the most terrible things in the collective enterprise of man. When, towards the end of the Second World War, we started to bomb the Germans into submission, we bombed Hamburg first, the city that had more anti-Nazi votes than any other German city. These anguishes are the facts of life as we find them in history.

There are no simple correlations. This does not mean that we will not pray for our loved ones in the hazards and tumults of history, when so frequently their destiny is a curious combination of the physical and the spiritual. We certainly will not stop praying for their health, particularly in view of what we know about psychosomatic characteristics in the human personality today. We will pray for the health of other people and pray for their healing.

This is the realm of history which is a vast middle ground between the realm of grace and the realm of nature. But ultimately, of course, our Christian faith lives in the realm of grace, in the realm of freedom. This is God's freedom and my freedom, beyond the structures of my body; the realm of grace where I know God and am persuaded, as St. Paul says, that he knows me.

In that realm, finally, all concern for immediate correlations and coherences and meanings falls away. The Christian faith stands in the sense of an ultimate meaning. We may be persuaded that God is on our side—not against somebody else—but on our side in this ultimate sense. We are "sure that neither death nor life, nor angels, nor principalities, nor things present, nor things to come, . . . will be able to separate us from the love of God in Christ Jesus our Lord."

It is on that level of meaning that the Christian faith makes sense. The lower levels are a threat, not only to the sense of the meaning of life, but finally to the morals of life. We must not deny that there is a kind of religion that enhances the ego and gives it an undue place in the world. But from the standpoint of our faith we should take our humble and contrite place in God's plan of the whole, and leave it to him to complete the fragmentation of our life.

O God, who has promised that all things will work together for good to those that love you, grant us patience amidst the tumults, pains and afflictions of life, and faith to discern your love, within, above, and beyond the impartial destinies of this great drama of life. Save us from every vainglorious pretension by which we demand favors which violate your love for all your children, and grant us grace to appropriate every fortune, both good and evil, for the triumph of the suffering, crucified, and risen Lord in our souls and life. In whose name we ask it.

3.   Prayers of Praise

Many, O Lord, are the wonderful works which you have wrought. They cannot be reckoned up in order. If we should declare and speak of them, they are more than we can number. We give praise for the creation of the world, for the majesty of the mountains and for the mighty deeps, for the myriad number of all your creatures, each sustaining its life according to the plan you have ordained. We give praise for the life of man, whom you have created in your image and called into fellowship with you, whom you have endowed with memory and foresight, so that all our yesterdays are gathered together in our present moment and all our tomorrows are the object of our hopes and apprehension.

O Lord, you have made us very great. Help us to remember how weak we are; so that we may not deny our kinship with the creatures of the field and our common dependence with them upon summer and winter, day and night. O Lord, you have made us very small, and we bring our years to an end like a tale that is told; help us to remember that beyond our brief day is the eternity of your love.

We praise you for the created world. We thank you for the creation, for we are fearfully and wonderfully made. Marvelous are your works, and that our soul knows well. We thank you for the world about us, which sustains us by its regular rhythm of summer and winter, of seedtime and harvest, and supplies us with our sustenance by the recurrent miracle of dying seed and growing plant, of dying flower and ripening fruit.

❦

In the beauty of this morning we give you thanks, O Lord, for life and love and the joy of existence, for the echo in human hearts to all pure and lovely things, for the promise of life and youth and the dawn of the unknown and for the hope and assurance of fulfillment. We rejoice in the glory of manhood and womanhood, in the innocence of children and the serene wisdom of age. We rejoice in the sweetness of companionship and in the joy of understanding hearts, in the faith of strong souls and the wholesomeness of simple people whom pride has not touched. We give you thanks for the pleasures of art and literature, for the enrichment of personality through every ministry of truth and beauty and goodness.

We confess that we are not worthy of the riches of life for which the generations of men have labored that we might enter into this heritage. We confess the sorry confusion of our common life, the greed which disfigures our collective life and sets man against his fellowmen. We confess the indifference and callousness with which we treat the sufferings and the insecurity of the poor, and the pettiness which mars the relations between us. May we with contrite hearts seek once more to purify our spirits, and to clarify our reason so that a fairer temple for the human spirit may be built in human society.

❦

Our Father, we welcome this new day with grateful hearts and thank you that the night yields to the day, and that you are Lord both of light and darkness. You have ordained a life of sleeping and waking, reminding us of of our frailty by our need of sleep, and of our greatness by the visions and responsibilities of the day. Though our day is short, you have permitted us to survey the ages in our brief hour, and to claim our kinship with the noble living and the noble dead, to find our own place in the long sad and majestic history of our race and to see our duties and responsibilities in ever-widening circles of human relations.

Grant us, our Father, grace to work while it is day, for the night comes when no man can work. Let our work be done this day with a sense of our responsibility to you in our several callings. Save us from sloth and waywardness. Keep us humble in your sight and before our fellowmen, so that neither pride nor indifference may destroy the bond which we have with our co-workers. May our love of you hallow all our relations, and our service to our fellows complete our reverent obedience.

Our Father, at the beginning of this new day we unite our prayers and aspirations with your children everywhere, and remember in our intercessions all sorts and conditions of men. Give your grace to all who are engaged in honorable toil, that they may enjoy their labors and garner the rightful fruits of their industry; save those who seek employment without avail from slothful resignation, and grant that as they resent the injustices from which they suffer, they may transmute resentment into an instrument of justice and may labor for a fairer world in which no one will want; endow those who are vested with authority with the spirit of humility so that pride may not corrupt them; give wisdom to all upon whose decisions hang the weal and woe of fellowmen; help each of us to see our task in its relation to your larger purpose that we may do it diligently and joyfully. Amend what flaws may lurk in our imperfect endeavors so that your strength may be made perfect in our weakness.

O Lord, great God and great king above all gods, we praise your majesty and your power. You have formed the earth and created man. Behind every mystery of life is the mystery of your power, and above every majesty is the majesty of your holiness. We praise you for your power which sustains all that is good and brings evil to naught, but even more for your mercy which recreates the wayward hearts of men. Your wrath casts down every high thing which exalts itself; but by your forgiveness you lift up those who are penitent of heart. Grant us grace to bring forth fruits meet for repentance.

O Lord, our God, how excellent is your name in all the world. You have laid the foundations of the earth; the heavens are the work of your hands; all things have their beginning in your almighty word, and their end in the glory of salvation.

We praise you for the special gifts you have bestowed on us above the rest of your creation. You have made us a little lower than the angels, and crowned our life with reason and imagination; so that we may survey the whole wide world; and also to sense and feel the mystery of what is beyond, and in worship to acknowledge that holiness which is the beginning and the end of the created world.

We thank you for this good earth and for all the dependable rhythms in this our natural home, which speaks to us of the constancy of your love: for the alternations of day and night, of seedtime and harvest; for the fruits of the earth and every miracle of abundance by which our life is sustained; for the daily round of our duties and the discipline of our responsibilities; for the rest which comes after toil at the end of the day and also at the end of our day of life.

We give you thanks that you have recreated us by your mercy as you have created us by your power. We praise you for every community of love where we are known and our lacks forgiven and for every ministry of grace where our offenses and the burden of an uneasy conscience, and also the frictions and resentments of life, are resolved in forgiveness and mercy.

Almighty and everlasting God, who created us by your power, and bears us in your mercy, we praise you for every revelation of your holiness above and beyond the transient majesties of our history. You are holy both in your power and in your goodness. Your power stands above all the majesties which we create in our image, changing the glory of the incorruptible God into the image of corruptible man. You are more powerful than we, and the order which you have established in your creation will bring to naught every vain thing which exalts itself above its measure. You are holy in your goodness, and the majesty of your mercy is greater than the majesty of your power. You have created us in your power but have redeemed us in the weakness of your love. We praise and magnify your name.

O Lord, our God, creator of the world and redeemer of men, we praise the majesty of your power and the greater majesty of your mercy. You have made the earth and created man, your hands stretched out the heavens and commanded all their hosts. You have commanded the morning and caused the dayspring to know his place. Great and wonderful are your works. Pity our weakness and subdue our pride that we may worship you with contrite hearts.

O Lord, the redeemer of men, who makes the wrath of man to praise you, who rules and overrules the angry passions and affections of men, we thank you that your mercy restores what human sin despoils. Grant us grace that our pride may be humbled and we may know him who can be known only in contrition. Save us from thinking of ourselves more highly than we ought to think. Cast down imaginations and every high thing which exalts itself. Knowing ourselves to be creatures, dependent upon your providence, help us to walk in faith. Knowing ourselves to be unrighteous, deserving your wrath, may we walk in humility before you. Knowing the richness of your mercy, save us from despair, and teach us to walk triumphantly, being persuaded that neither life nor death, angels nor principalities; not height nor depth, nor things present nor things to come nor any other creature shall be able to separate us from the love of God.

O Judge of the world, whose holiness reveals all our righteousnesses as filthy rags, whose thoughts are not our thoughts and whose ways are not our ways, who makes the judges of the world as vanity, who resists the proud and gives grace to the humble, we worship you. In your majesty and goodness, all human virtue is at once fulfilled and annulled.

O God, the redeemer of the world, who takes no delight in the death of the wicked but desires that all men come to the knowledge of life, who in Christ has suffered with us, and through whom you have taken the chastisement of our peace upon yourself, we worship you who are the fountain of mercy, and whose majesty is the majesty of love.

4. We See Through a Glass Darkly

Though I speak with the tongues of men and of angels, and have not love, I am become as sounding brass, or a tinkling cymbal. And though I have the gift of prophecy and understand all mysteries, and all knowledge; and though I have all faith, so that I could remove mountains, and have not love, I am nothing. And though I bestow all my goods to feed the poor, and though I give my body to be burned, and have not love, it profiteth me nothing.

Love suffereth long, and is kind; love envieth not; love vaunteth not itself, is not puffed up, doth not behave itself unseemly, seeketh not her own, is not easily provoked, thinketh no evil; rejoiceth not in iniquity, but rejoiceth in the truth; beareth all things, believeth all things, hopeth all things, endureth all things.

Love never faileth: but whether there be prophecies, they shall fail; whether there be tongues, they shall cease; whether there be knowledge, it shall vanish away. For we know in part, and we prophesy in part. But when that which is perfect is come, then that which is in part shall be done away. When I was a child, I spake as a child, I understood as a child, I thought as a child: but when I became a man, I put away childish things. For now we see through a glass, darkly; but then face to face: now I know in part; but then shall I know even as also I am known. And now abideth faith, hope, love, these three; but the greatest of these is love.

I Corinthians 13

St. George's Church, New York, January 17, 1960. The Scripture is the Authorized Version, but using "love" rather than "charity" for the Greek *agape*.

It is still close enough to the New Year to choose from the New Testament lesson of the morning a topic that deals with the rapidity of change, the obscurity of the future, and the things that abide. So I take as my text the last words of this hymn of love of St. Paul in the thirteenth chapter of Corinthians: "We see through a glass darkly." St. Paul is saying there are so many changes that take place as time moves from the present to the future; prophecies shall change and perhaps pass away; all the new circumstances of life make these forms of knowledge and prophecy irrelevant. Then he talks about the three things that abide—faith, hope, love—and the greatest of these is love. This theme of St. Paul is what we shall consider.

We see through a glass darkly. How darkly? We know so much about the past, or think we know. Histories are piled upon histories, and we have some knowledge of the strange drama of the past. But no amount of knowledge or prophecy can predict the future. St. Paul was quite right: all these prophecies have proved to be vain. They will cease, as knowledge will cease. About these changing circumstances and therefore the transience of our knowledge and prophecy, let us take a look at just two things—the destiny of our whole civilization and our own private and family destiny. In this congregation there are families in all stages of growth and age, including children and parents. In regard to our family destinies, all we know is that we as parents decrease, our children increase, and that there comes a time in life when we face death. All we can do is to look at our children —sometimes with anxiety—and hope that we have not done them too much harm, and maybe a little good. We hope, perhaps, that they will have some touches of their parents, but we know that they will be their own persons and that they must make their own way. Our knowledge is not able to anticipate their future, and we have to have confidence in the freedom of their persons. We may hope, by the grace of God, that they will weather the storms of life, the choice of vocation and all the other hazards of life, a little better than we did. This is how our knowledge is fragmentary, and we look through a glass darkly when we talk about our own private destinies.

But what about our collective destiny as a nation? Nothing is more certain than the ever-increasing rapidity of historical change that has made all knowledge and prophecy of no avail. They will vanish away, as St. Paul says. Here is this great nation. We started out with the faith of our founding fathers which is, in a way, our liberal democratic faith. It has something that abides in it; but it is very individualistic. It did not anticipate a civilization where we maintain a tolerable justice by fantastically complex equilibria of power; it did not anticipate big business, big labor, collectivism. We are not Communist, but we have forms of collectivism all the same. So a new insight has to take the place of the old insight if we are going to have a tolerable community. Our nation has a very peculiar past because it was rocked in the cradle of continental security and seemed omnipotent in the day of its impotence. Because it was impotent, there were many things that it could not do. Now we find ourselves vaulted to the position of seeming omnipotence. Yet in this omnipotence we can do less of what we want to do than we could in the day of our seeming impotence. This is a tremendous change that no human knowledge and no human prophecy could calculate, for prophecy and knowledge pass away. To make matters more confounded, we tried to divide the world according to the dogmas of the so-called cold war. In that period all the prophecies of our world and the Communist world proved that they pass away.

Much of the wisdom of the Western world looked for meaning in terms of progress. Man hoped for improvement in education, in human understanding or social organization, and prophecies abounded as to the wonderful quality and shape of the future. But instead we are caught in the nuclear dilemma. These prophecies have also passed away. The transience of life itself makes for the transience of human knowledge and human prophecy. Note how St. Paul emphasized the fragmentary character of all human knowledge. There are many forms of Christian faith and many forms of secularism that are not so modest. But if we do not recognize the fragmentary character of knowledge we will be caught holding onto some old form of knowledge which is quite irrelevant to the responsibilities which we must face today. So much for the transience which attends our community and the whole world situation and the transience of our knowledge.

Over against this, St. Paul emphasized the faith that abides. "Now abideth faith, hope, love, these three; but the greatest of these is love." So let us consider these three things that abide. It is important to analyze the character of the Christian faith in terms of faith, hope, and love, because some of our non-Christian friends say that is where the Christian faith becomes sentimental. What abides is just an attitude toward life, but what is an attitude against all these tremendous vicissitudes? In what sense do faith, hope, and love, abide?

Let us first consider faith. In any one of these three there is always the possibility of a childish quality that must be overcome. Even in faith, hope, and love there must be some development from childhood to maturity. St. Paul says, "When I was a child, I spoke like a child and I thought like a child;. . .when I became a man, I gave up childish ways." Now in the Bible faith does not mean belief in something probably, but not absolutely, true. Nor is it belief in something that is quite incredible from the standpoint of the rational man. No, faith means trust. The late Middleton Murray described it as trust that there is a meaning and a purpose beyond all our fragmentary purposes. Or as St. Paul expresses it, "Ultimately, I will know what I do not know now, and even if I do not know, I am known." This is faith in an overall, overreaching purpose of meaning. This, for some of us, is the central emphasis of the Christian and the whole biblical idea of faith-as-trust. Trust in God also means trust in life itself, despite the obvious patches of meaninglessness which sometimes drive us to the

edge of despair. If we do not admit that these patches of meaninglessness are there, then our faith becomes sentimental. It also means that
we should not expect the drama of history to be played for the sake
of *our* security, or for the security of *our* nation or the security of
our civilization.

Recently there appeared a collection of letters between two of our
founding fathers, Thomas Jefferson and John Adams. These men were
rather close friends, but became by the exigencies of politics during
the Washington administration leaders of the Democratic and the
Federalist parties. Despite the animosity of political conflict, they
reestablished their friendship in their old age, and exchanged awfully
good sense, and nonsense, in these letters about life, mutual friends,
faith, and the character of faith. Jefferson was a kind of Christian,
influenced by deist rationalism. He wrote to Adams that he was a
Christian in the only sense that Christ, so he thought, would admit
discipleship. He believed in universal benevolence, which comes quite
close to that final phrase in our text, "Now the greatest of these is
love." But this was not enough for Adams. He said religious faith
must mean something more than that. So Jefferson asked what it did
mean. Adams gave a classical answer. He said, faith means that I
rejoice in God and his creation, and I exult in my own existence. As
I read this I thought that the final phrase sounded somewhat heretical.
Yet, the psalmist says, "I am fearfully and wonderfully made: marvelous are thy works; and that my soul knoweth right well." This is
classical Christian faith against the childish corruption of that faith.

If it be not regarded as sentimental, I would like to refer to a good
friend of mine, the late senior warden of this church,* whom I miss
in his usual seat in the front pew. He illustrated to me the maturity
of Christian faith. There was no sentimentality in his faith at all. There
was no "lobbying in the courts of the Almighty for special favors,"

*Charles Burlingham.

to use William James's phrase. He was almost a discarnate spirit as he grew blind and deaf, and he looked on his blindness and his deafness with a touch of humor and impatience but not with despair, and upon the possibility of his death as a form of release and triumph. We might think also of Albert Camus, the Nobel Prize-winning French novelist who lost his life in an automobile accident just a week or two ago. He was described in many of the obituary notices as a leading French existentialist. But he himself had denied he was an existentialist. As a matter of fact, he was partly a Christian believer and partly an agnostic. He was an agnostic because he said, "I think death is absurd." There is irony in the fact that he died in the most absurd way in an automobile driven by his friend at ninety miles an hour. But why should anybody, an intelligent man, or anyone, say that death is so absurd? For it is one of the things that belongs to our existence. "As dying, and behold, we live," says St. Paul. There must be a quality of faith that takes in the curious paradox of life that man has such a great dignity and is yet so miserable in his anxiety about death and, furthermore, knows that he ought not to be. Christian faith is no sentimental thing. It is a faith that takes all the dimensions of life into consideration, including in Pascal's phrase, "not only the dignity of man, but the misery of man." Such a faith affirms that despite all these paradoxes, patches of meaninglessness, and tragedies, man can, in the words of John Adams, "rejoice in God and his creation."

Now there abideth hope. Hope is a particular form of faith; hope is faith related to the future. Hope can be as egoistic as faith in that we face the same problems of immaturity and maturity. Thus, we might hope that our nation will always be as great as it is now, or we might hope that an umbrella of security will be established over our family against all other families; or we might hope that Western civilization will survive untouched and that Communism will perish. Those forms of hope are not really mature hope. To have mature hope is to rejoice in the whole drama of human history, including the terrible anxieties of a nuclear age. We do not know whether we will survive or whether the great powers will destroy each other in their fateful struggle on the abyss of nuclear annihilation. But we hope that we have the wisdom and responsibility to escape this fate, in which case we could have a more universal community. In a sense we are saved by hope, in that we believe not only in the goodness of life, but we believe in the meaningfulness of the great drama of life. This is the distinctive point of what we call biblical religion. Biblical religion is distinguished from all Oriental and classical religions in that it does not regard history as meaningless but believes that something happens in history that is important. We do not have to flee from history into eternity, but eternity is a quality which is gained by faith and love in history. So now abideth faith and hope.

And finally, as St. Paul says, there "abideth love"—and "the greatest of these is love." It is very important that St. Paul should have said this. Thomas Jefferson said that Jesus had an ethic of pure benevolence. But Paul, in this hymn of love, captures the spirit of what Jefferson called Jesus' sense of universal benevolence. "The greatest of these is love." When we talk about love, we have to become mature or we will become sentimental. Let us not say that we as Christians are potential martyrs, or that we are more unselfish than other people. That is not what love means if we take it modestly. Basically, love means that life has no meaning except in terms of responsibility; responsibility toward our family, toward our nation, toward our civilization and, now, by the pressures of history, toward the universe of mankind which includes our enemies. "The greatest of these is love" —"Thou shall love thy neighbor as thyself"—that is the basic meaning of love, as the permanent, abiding value of life.

There is always a possibility of realizing two pinnacles of love above this basic meaning. One pinnacle is sacrificial love, which is called the sign of the cross by Christopher Dawson, a distinguished Catholic philosopher, in a recent book on the history of Western civilization. Dawson makes the statement that Christianity lives by the sign of the cross, or Christian civilization lives by the sign of the cross, while modern civilization lives by the sign of the dollar. There is a certain pretentiousness about this claim for Christianity, particularly when the author refers to the first great Christian emperor, Constantine, who "invented" the sign of the cross, for it appeared to him in a dream when he battled against his foe for the supremacy of the Roman Empire. But this same Constantine committed three murders, including the murder of his wife, in order to reach the precarious eminence of the imperial throne. Should not the cross stand as the symbol of real sacrificial love? We cannot dismiss the fact that there must be sacrificial love as an abiding value of life.

We know, however, that business and politics are not governed by unselfishness. All the justice we have is a justice which has transmuted the sense of responsibility in various balances of power in order to prevent the strong from taking advantage of the weak, by making the weak a little stronger but not too strong. Always we are dealing with sinful man. This pinnacle of sacrifice must be looked at carefully. We know that sacrificial love is the pattern of life which the martyrs have illustrated.

Another pinnacle of love in the New Testament is very important —love as forgiveness. "Be kindly affectioned one with another," says St. Paul in another one of his epistles, "forgiving one another, even as God also in Christ forgives you." A secular friend recently suggested that he did not like the idea of forgiveness because there was an element of condescension in it, for the righteous person forgave the sinners. If there be such an element in it, it is thoroughly unscriptural because everything in the New Testament advises that we cannot forgive one another if we think ourselves more righteous than the other. All forgiveness really comes down, particularly in the family, to mutual forbearance, perhaps best expressed in a certain sense of humor. Probably no happy family has ever existed purely by a sense of justice. If you live absolutely by a sense of justice it could be from one perspective that the man gives more than the woman, and from another perspective that the woman gives more than the man. How are you going to solve this, except by mutual forbearance? When that mutual forbearance is lacking, the family ties can break.

There is always a chance of an immature expression of what St. Paul calls "childish things" in each of these abiding values. But as we have it in our biblical teachings and as we experience it in life, these abide even when prophecies and knowledge cease to be. "Now abideth faith, hope, love, these three."

Eternal God, Father Almighty, maker of heaven and earth, we worship you. Your wisdom is beyond our understanding, your power is greater than we can measure, your thoughts are above our thoughts; as high as the heaven is above the earth, your majesty judges all human majesties. Your judgment brings princes to naught, and makes the judges of the earth as vanity; for before the mountains were brought forth or ever the earth and the world were made, even from everlasting to everlasting you are God.

Give us grace to apprehend by faith the power and wisdom which lie beyond our understanding; and in worship to feel that which we do not know, and to praise even what we do not understand; so that in the presence of your glory we may be humble, and in the knowledge of your judgment we may repent; and so in the assurance of your mercy, we may rejoice and be glad.

5. Law, Conscience, and Grace

Therefore you have no excuse, O man, whoever you are, when you judge another; for in passing judgment upon him you condemn yourself, because you, the judge, are doing the very same things. We know that the judgment of God rightly falls upon those who do such things. Do you suppose, O man, that when you judge those who do such things and yet do them yourself, you will escape the judgment of God? Or do you presume upon the riches of his kindness and forbearance and patience? Do you not know that God's kindness is meant to lead you to repentance? But by your hard and impenitent heart you are storing up wrath for yourself on the day of wrath when God's righteous judgment will be revealed. For he will render to every man according to his works: to those who by patience in well-doing seek for glory and honor and immortality, he will give eternal life; but for those who are factious and do not obey the truth, but obey wickedness, there will be wrath and fury. There will be tribulation and distress for every human being who does evil, the Jew first and also the Greek, but glory and honor and peace for every one who does good, the Jew first and also the Greek. For God shows no partiality.

All who have sinned without the law will also perish without the law, and all who have sinned under the law will be judged by the law. For it is not the hearers of the law who are righteous before God, but the doers of the law who will be justified. When Gentiles who have not the law do by nature what the law requires, they are a law to themselves, even though they do not have the law. They show that what the law

St. George's Church, New York, February 19, 1961.

requires is written on their hearts, while their conscience also bears
witness and their conflicting thoughts accuse or perhaps excuse them
on that day when, according to my gospel, God judges the secrets of men
by Christ Jesus.

Romans 2:1–16, RSV

"When Gentiles who have not the law do by nature what the law
requires, they are a law to themselves, . . . while their conscience also
bears witness and their conflicting thoughts accuse or perhaps excuse
them." This passage from the Scripture lesson of the morning follows
a long disquisition by St. Paul in the first and second chapters of the
Epistle to the Romans about self-examination, which is a proper topic
for the first Sunday in Lent. St. Paul's argument is that we all stand
under an ultimate judgment, and that ultimate judgment is more
severe than we might think because we regard ourselves as fairly
virtuous, but we are not ultimately or absolutely virtuous.

Many critics of our religious life are apt to say that people have an
uneasy conscience because they have violated some arbitrary law.
This may be true, for there are many arbitrary and some fantastic laws
that have been set up in the ages of religious history. But St. Paul's
point is that this uneasy conscience belongs to the nature of our
existence. The "Gentiles who have not the law," that is, no external
code, no commandments, yet "do by nature what the law requires,"
and "show that what the law requires is written in their heart, while
their conscience also bears witness and their conflicting thoughts
accuse or perhaps excuse them." This last remark, echoing a well-
known Stoic postulate, is psychologically very acute. What is our
conscience? Conscience can be defined as the self looking at itself. It
gets its standards from what is written into its own nature. Now our
own nature is that we cannot be ourselves only within ourselves. Man
is too great and too small, and his greatness cannot be contained in
his smallness. The self always goes out from itself in affections, re-

sponsibilities, and engagements. The self always returns to itself. And
on the whole we have a feeling that going out from oneself is creative,
and that returning to oneself is destructive.

So that is why, in our moments of self-examination, we have this
ambivalence, our conscience or our self-awareness accusing, or else
excusing, us. One time we say, "Well, what a horrible, selfish person
I am. I didn't realize how selfish I have been." And the next time we
say, "You know, considering and comparing myself with other people, I really am, after all, not so bad." Excusing ourselves, the uneasi-
ness about this never stops. There is a reason for that. It is because
the ambivalence in our character never stops, so that we never can be
regarded as mainly virtuous or mainly not virtuous. The human situation makes it natural for us to go out from ourselves: "For whosoever
seeketh to gain his life will lose it, but whoso loseth his life will find
it." That is the basic law of human existence, and the one impulse in
life. The other impulse is always to draw all life into ourselves. While
there are relativities of good and evil, we all have a sense of universal
law, and we know that a consistent self-regard is evil and that a
consistent self-forgetfulness is good. For life is not made up of consistent self-regard and consistent self-forgetfulness. Rather, there is the
antiphonal movement, the dialectic between going out from oneself
and returning to oneself. When we examine our lives, on any level, we
find our consciences accusing or else excusing us.

Take, for instance, the family relation. What is more virtuous than
the love of parents for their children? The love of parents for their
children is a virtuous going out from ourselves. It is one of the ways
of grace that overcomes our selfishness; that we fall in love, that we
found families, that we love our mates and we love our children. We
think we are virtuous. Looking at our virtue, we say, "I am a good
parent." Probably we are not as good as we think we are. Our children
may not have the same complacent judgment about us. And they may
be good children, they may not be even rebellious. They are just trying

to establish themselves, and they detect, without being psychiatrists, that there is a curious combination of possessiveness with our love, particularly if we are good parents. Psychiatrists say: "Children have problems, but their chief problem is parents." A mother's love, a parent's love, has this peculiar amalgam of going out from oneself and returning to oneself. We love our children. If they are bright, we are proud of them. This is always the dialectic of love in the family relationship.

There is in the world of human affairs the creativity of scientists, scholars, businessmen, and public officials. As far as they are engaged in their responsibilities and striving for excellence, this is virtue, this is creativity. They well may excuse themselves and say, "Look what I have done for people." But each of us has got where we are not merely by the pull of responsibilities, but by the push of ambition.

There is an interesting ambiguity in the words ambition and ambitious. Sometimes when we praise a man we say he is very ambitious. Sometimes when we condemn him we say he is very ambitious. Is being ambitious a virtue or a vice? Probably it is both, because ambition contains the urge to be excellent in your field or discipline. It also contains the urge to get ahead of other people! Academics, and probably also clergy, are apt to be critical of politicians who are obviously ambitious. We are all ambitious, and we are all jealous of somebody else who has a greater eminence. The politician happens to display his ambition more publicly than anybody else. Always, it comes back to accusing or excusing ourselves.

In our collective life, there will be more accusing and less excusing, for we cannot deny that however virtuous and unselfish we are as individuals, collectively we are and have been selfish. Collective egotism, particularly the collective arrogance of the races, is tremendous. Even that, however, is not pure evil, when one recalls what the white man's civilization has done for Africa, for example, which is now forgotten by the black African states. But why do we taint these creativities of our Western civilization with obvious arrogance that has made the white man odious on the black continent?

In our collective activities there is egotism in regard to race and perhaps to class, and certainly in regard to our own nation. Not only our enemies or detractors, but our friends and allies, are inclined to say that we think too highly of ourselves. Collectively we excuse and do not accuse ourselves, because from the day of our founding we have had the idea that we are a peculiarly virtuous nation. Other nations are selfish, but we are not. We stand for justice and freedom, not for self-interest. It is basically impossible for a nation so to do. Nations more than individuals think about their own interests, and we ought to realize that if we have any virtue, it is not pure unselfishness but the virtue of a relative justice that finds a point of concurrence between our interests and those of the larger world.

This is the situation in human nature. Whether in the family or in the nation, there is always a mixture of good and evil, of self-regard and self-giving, of self-obsession and self-forgetfulness.

There are many answers to this problem. One is the answer of complacence which says, "Well, that's the way we are. We are all selfish—what of that?" Montaigne, the great Renaissance philosopher said, "I know my nature. I want to be just as I am. . . . I don't strive with my nature." Did he mean to say—"I do not strive with my nature of self-regarding. I want to be just what I am"?

If you don't strive with it at all, your self-regard gets to be so consistent that it borders on neurosis. A more popular answer is to pretend that we are not self-regarding, that we really are interested in other people. Since we always are interested in others to some degree, we can make that point. Pretension is one of the evils of all good people. A brilliant English philosopher in a book that has not been widely enough read, *Principles of Power,** declared: "If people

*Philip Leon.

deceive their fellowmen about their motives, they are doing it just because they first want to deceive themselves and use their fellowmen as allies of their self-deception." This again is the curious business of accusing and excusing ourselves. We have a deep suspicion that we are more concerned with ourselves than we ought to be, therefore, we try to make ourselves appear a little better.

The third answer involves an ascetic position, which has a great tradition. We *are* self-regarding. Very well, we will do everything to *root* out this self from itself. We will be selfless, utterly selfless. The Protestant Reformation revolted against these disciplines of unselfish asceticism. Mystic asceticism is the self trying to get rid of itself. There is the well-known mystic saying, "The self is like an onion with layer upon layer of self-regard that has to be peeled off." But others have pointed out that it is impossible to get rid of the self by peeling off layers of self-regard, for the self, like the onion, only becomes more and more pungent.

Finally, there is a healthy, but not cynical, realism about our selfishness. Martin Luther said—and this is frequently misunderstood—"Sin bravely, if also you have great faith." This means, don't be so morbid about the fact that you're selfish; don't deny that you are self-regarding, but work in life and hope that by grace—this perhaps is the door to the real answer—you will be redeemed. *By grace.*

Today even Christians do not emphasize common grace enough. We do not become unselfish by saying so. But, thank God, there are forces in life and in history that draw us out of ourselves and make us truly ourselves. This is grace: common grace, prevenient grace. Grace is every impulse or power which operates against the pull of my self-regard, and makes me truly a self by helping me to forget myself. This is the basic answer of the Christian faith.

Certain other answers follow. One is that if this is a permanent situation, then there is a chance that you can change. It may be a change wrought by some destiny of history, of affection and responsibility, whether in family, in community, or in state. Perhaps we should draw the conclusion that our common life, particularly among the nations, is made tolerable by the knowledge of all this. We are sufferable only when somebody has the power and the courage to stand against us.

The history of Western democracy and the pageant of its development rest upon this insight about common grace. An English historian once said: "Modern democracy rests upon the insight that what I think to be just is tainted by my own self-interest. I have just enough residual virtue to know that it *is* tainted, and that someone has to stand against me, and declare his different conviction."

All our justice rests upon, on the one hand, a political elaboration of our mutualities; and on the other hand, upon elaboration of delicate balances of power that prevent us from being as self-regarding as we might be.

The second insight answers other questions about the problem of self. It is that we should try to be as rigorous in judging ourselves as we are in the judging of others, which we never are, of course. It is the answer of forgiveness. St. Paul puts the whole of human life in the context of a great drama of divine forgiveness. "And be kind to one another, forgiving one another as God in Christ forgave you." We must move from the nicely calculated less or more of how good or how selfish we are, to the recognition instead that we all stand in the need of forgiveness. "Forgive us our sins; our trespasses or debts, sins of commission or omission; as we forgive those who sin against us." The important word is *as*—we forgive.

Forgiving one another does not mean a condescending forgiveness of the virtuous man for the unvirtuous man. It means that no one can forgive who does not know that he is tainted with the same self-regard as the person he is forgiving.

How could our family life exist without this? Family life begins by the impulse of nature, two people meeting each other, falling in love with each other. But as they live together, something more grows up which is of the matter of the spirit, ultimately what the New Testament calls reconciliation, mutual forgiveness, mutual forbearance. Sometimes this can be done by a little sense of humor rather than some obvious form of reconciliation. But constant reconciliation goes on in the sense that we know we hurt each other even when we try not to, or that we hurt our children or that they hurt us; and yet we continue bearing and forbearing with each other with, we hope, more understanding. Thank God for the ultimate redemption where there is forgiveness of sin.

The creed ends with the promise, "I believe . . . in the forgiveness of sins; and . . . life everlasting." What would life everlasting be without the forgiveness of our sins to each other?

Father of all mercies, teach us to be merciful as you are merciful. Father of all forgiveness, help us to forgive others as you have forgiven us.

Grant, O Lord, to the living, grace; to the church and to all mankind, peace and concord; to us and all your servants, life everlasting.

6. Prayers of Worship and Thanksgiving

Almighty God, Father of mercies and fountain of all goodness, we praise you for all your gifts to us and to all men. We thank you for our life and for the blessings of health and strength; we thank you for all the affections and love we meet in our daily life, for all the responsibilities which relate us to those around us; help us to extend our concern to those afar off, and make us mindful that we have been given means of doing good.

We give thanks for every measure by which you have taught us your truth and have brought our life into conformity with your will. Multiply your grace in us. We ask that no ignorance or sin may turn your blessings into curses. Give us such a lively sense of your goodness that we may devote ourselves to your will and service, so that, loving you, we may find the way to an increasing love and brotherly communion with all your children.

O God, who has made all things by your power, ruler of the world and redeemer of men, and who is more wonderful in your majesty than we can know, and in your mercy than we can understand, we worship you, the author of all life, the preserver of men, and the redeemer of the world.

We thank you for the life and joy in your whole creation, for the rhythm of its seasons, for the rigor of its disciplines, for the miracle of abundance by which we are sustained, for the creatures great and small in whom you have revealed your life-giving power, for the warmth of the day and the quiet of the night, for the work which follows rest and the rest which follows work, and for all the alternations by which you temper the rigors of life to the frailty of man.

We thank you for the fellowship of men under your providence, for the structure of life by which you have ordained that none of us should live alone. We thank you for our families and our responsibilities toward each other, and for the bond between youth and age; for our communities of common interest and work, in which we discipline each other in our mutual tasks; for the large communities of destiny into which we are bound in our nations; and finally for our common dependence on and responsibility to the family of nations. We thank you for every discipline which teaches us that if we try to gain our life we lose it, but if we lose it in service to our fellows we find it.

Almighty God, creator of the world, we worship the majesty of your power. We praise you for the constancy of your providence, revealed in the ordered course of nature and the rhythm of summer and winter, day and night. We praise you too for the richness of creation, for all the creatures great and small and for your providence which rules over all creation.

We worship you as the Lord of our spirits and our history; you have created us in your image, endowed us with freedom, and when we use that freedom to defy your will, you contrive by every stern measure of justice and every guile of mercy to reclaim us. How marvelous are your works in the history of man, how terrible your judgments, and yet how merciful your goodness to those who are of contrite heart.

Hear us as we commit our lives to you this day. Bless the work done in this place today so that all who labor and learn here may walk worthy of the vocation wherewith they are called, with all lowliness and meekness, endeavoring to keep the unity of the spirit in the bond of peace. Give us grace to be members together in one body, each member serving the whole. Help us also to bestow the more abundant honor upon those members deemed less honorable so that we will not forget our dependence upon those whose humble duties make our life tolerable and free us for our own tasks.

We pray for the whole of our suffering humanity. We remember those who brave peril for our security. Succor all those who suffer, and sustain those who are driven to despair by hunger, imprisonment, oppression, and persecution. Remind us of our dignity as your children so that cowardice may not betray us into connivance with injustice. Remind us of our sins so that pride will not corrupt the justice which we must defend.

O Lord, who are able to make the wrath of man to praise you, rule and overrule the angry passions and sinful affections of men so that we may be led out of this night of sorrow and sin into a new day.

Almighty Father, who are the source and the end of our life and the light also of our pilgrimage, grant your grace so that the good in us may prevail over the evil, so that everything in us may be brought in harmony with your will, and we may be enabled to live in charity with our neighbors and fellow workers.

O Lord, who are the confidence of all the ends of the earth and the refuge of your children in all generations, enlarge our faith and love so that we may pray truly for needs beyond our own. We pray for our country and its leaders; keep them on the paths of justice. We pray for your Church throughout the world and for all the ministers of your mercy, that each may serve you more truly according to his vocation. We pray for those who work with their hands, that they may know the dignity of their work. We pray for those who care for the young, that they may not cause any of the little ones to stumble. More particularly, we pray for the millions of distressed and dispossessed, anguished souls who have been uprooted by the storms and tumults of war. O Lord, save us from heedlessness in a world full of sorrow, and from self-righteousness, for in our world, the sins of even the most wicked trace some kinship with the sins of even the most righteous. Cover us all by your mercy, and lead us to a fuller understanding of your will.

O God, who has taught us to pray for the coming of your kingdom on this earth, give us grace to build our communities after the fashion of your kingdom, to set no boundaries around them which you would not set, to quiet the tumult within them by brotherly love and to work the more diligently for the better concord in them, because our final security lies in the city which has foundations, whose builder and maker is God.

Almighty God, our Father, we worship you, the creator of the world and the redeemer of men.

We praise your power and your might. Before the mountains were brought forth or ever the earth and the world were made, even from everlasting to everlasting, you are God, while we bring our years to an end like a tale that is told.

We praise you for your goodness and your mercy. You have both formed and reformed, both created and recreated us. We are fearfully and wonderfully made; marvelous are your works, and that our soul knows well. Your forgiveness and mercy have released us from the pains of an unquiet conscience and freed us to become co-workers together with you. We thank you for all your mercies.

Grant us grace, our Father, to serve you in our several callings. May the ministers of your gospel rightly divide the word of truth. May all doctors and nurses and other ministers of mercy be fit instruments of your healing grace. May all who serve in the market places of the world seek to do justice and refrain from all fraud. We pray especially for all who brave great peril in our behalf. Give them a sense of high calling in their duties, that they may know whose majesty they finally serve and may be courageous in conflict and humble in the hour of victory. Bless all who guide our children and every minister of knowledge and truth. O Lord, who has given us diversities of gifts but the same spirit and differences of administration under the same Lord, help us to be members one of another and to acknowledge your will as our law in all our doings.

O Almighty God, who alone can order the unruly wills and affections of sinful men, grant unto your people that they may love the thing which you command, and desire that which you promise, so that, among the sundry and manifold changes of this world, our hearts may surely be fixed where true joys are to be found.

We pray for all who are set in authority over us, and who make decisions in our behalf. Endow them with the spirit of justice and teach them to seek your wisdom when the perplexities they face are more than their own wisdom can resolve.

7. The Wheat and the Tares

Lord, thou hast been our dwelling place in all
  generations.
Before the mountains were brought forth,
  or ever thou hadst formed the earth and the world,
  even from everlasting to everlasting, thou art God.

Thou turnest man to destruction;
  and sayest, Return, ye children of men.
For a thousand years in thy sight
  are but as yesterday when it is past,
  and as a watch in the night.

Thou carriest them away as with a flood; they are as a sleep:
  in the morning they are like grass which groweth up.
In the morning it flourisheth, and groweth up;
  in the evening it is cut down, and withereth.

For we are consumed by thine anger,
  and by thy wrath are we troubled.
Thou has set our iniquities before thee,
  our secret sins in the light of thy countenance.

For all our days are passed away in thy wrath:
  we spend our years as a tale that is told.
The days of our years are threescore years and ten;
  and if by reason of strength they be fourscore years,
yet is their strength labour and sorrow;
  for it is soon cut off, and we fly away.

Psalm 90:1–10, AV

Union Theological Seminary, New York, February 28, 1960.

*Another parable put he forth unto them, saying, The kingdom of
heaven is likened unto a man which sowed good seed in his field: But
while men slept, his enemy came and sowed tares among the wheat, and
went his way. But when the blade was sprung up, and brought forth
fruit, then appeared the tares also. So the servants of the householder
came and said unto him, Sir, didst not thou sow good seed in thy field?
from whence then hath it tares? He said unto them, An enemy hath
done this. The servants said unto him, Wilt thou then that we go and
gather them up? But he said, Nay; lest while ye gather up the tares, ye
root up also the wheat with them. Let both grow together until the
harvest: and in the time of harvest I will say to the reapers, Gather ye
together first the tares, and bind them in bundles to burn them: but
gather the wheat into my barn.*

                                                    Matthew 13:24–30, AV

I want to begin my sermon with the well-known ninetieth Psalm,
and end it with the parable of the wheat and the tares, which is the
New Testament lesson of the morning. The ninetieth Psalm begins
with the words, "Lord, Thou hast been our dwelling place in all
generations. Before the mountains were brought forth, or ever thou
hadst formed the earth and the world, even from everlasting to everlasting, Thou art God." Then it goes on to describe the human situation in typically biblical terms. "Thou carriest them (that is, us) away
as with a flood; . . . In the morning they are like grass which groweth
up. In the morning it flourisheth; . . . in the evening it is cut down
and withereth." The brevity of human life! "Thou carriest them away
as with a flood." We are like corks that bob up and down in the river
of time. The brevity of human life may fill us with melancholy because
it seems to reduce life to such insignificance. We bring our years to
an end like a tale that is told, says the Psalmist.

The second point in the analysis of the human situation is implicit
rather than explicit. Man is indeed like a cork that is drawn down the
river of time, carried away as with a flood. But he could not be

altogether that, because he knows about it; he speculates about it as the Psalmist does, and about the significance of it. Man stands outside of the river of time, so that he can anticipate his death either with hope or with melancholy. Also he can create. He is not only a creature, but he is a creator because he is not quite in the river of time; although he might forget how much of a creature he is when he begins to create. Therefore we come to the third point.

This drama of human history is indeed partly our construct, but it stands under a sovereignty much greater than ours. "A thousand years are in thy sight but as yesterday when it is past, and as a watch in the night." The drama of our individual life and the whole drama of human history stands under a mysterious and eternal sovereignty. It is a mysterious sovereignty which the prophets are always warning that we must not spell out too much. "My thoughts are not your thoughts, my ways are not your ways." But it is not complete mystery because—and this is the distinction between the biblical view and the philosophical view—in spite of the mystery, there are also glints of meaning in it. This God is the mysterious creator of the world, but he is also a just and merciful God.

The New Testament adds to this story by suggesting there is a clue to the mystery. This is the light that shineth in darkness, the drama of the life of our Lord Jesus Christ. Here we have a sense that the mystery of God's creativity and the mystery of his severe judgment and the mystery of his mercy are related, and the clue to the mystery lies in the combination of his justice and his mercy. How are they related; this is our question, and how are these all brought together and revealed? The light that shineth in darkness enables us to live our life, not merely in the sense of its brevity, but with a sense of a purpose for it, and also with the sense of a purpose, and judgment and ultimate fulfillment beyond any judgments or fulfillments that we can envisage.

There are various alternatives—modern and ancient—to what the biblical faith tells us about our human story. One of the great alternatives Aldous Huxley has defined as the "perennial philosophy," which many modern intellectuals, when they become religious, think is a plausible alternative to biblical faith.

According to this alternative view of life, attention is fastened on the second part of the human situation; man is in the river of time but is transcendent over it. This transcendence of his is indeterminate. He can rise higher and higher, and he can look at the whole thing and ask whether it has any meaning. Let him, therefore, rise higher and higher until he, in a sense, meets God. This is the strategy of detachment, according to which we all have our private airplanes, spiritually speaking, and these spiritual airplanes have indeterminate altitude records. There is no limit to how high you can go. You start, and raise yourself up from the human scene to the point where at first it seems creative, because you see, and are apologetic for, all your vanities and pretensions. You rise a little higher, and then you become apologetic for anything that you have done responsibly and creatively. And then you also begin to look at your fellowmen, and you see mothers caring for their children, scholars engaged in their enterprises, businessmen in the marketplace, politicians fighting for their causes, and you say, "What is the good of this? This is all in the river of time. This is all so brief, and also it may be corrupt."

Playing God to the universe, in other words, can be very exhilarating but very irresponsible. It it a strategy of weakness rather than of strength; if you happen to be very weak, you can look at the world from the highest altitude you can think of. If you get high enough in an airplane, you know that the farm of the good farmer and of the bad farmer look equally like garden plots. All distinctions disappear. All moral responsibilities disappear. Indeterminate extension of our freedom over time is certainly no answer to the problem of life.

Probably not many Christians are tempted to this alternative, yet it is a perennial temptation through the ages; if you would have a religious census of the world you would find that more people than the Christians or the Jews have some vision of this alternative to biblical religion.

Which brings us now again to the strategy of life as we have it in the faith of the Bible. We look at the brevity of our life. We admit that we are creatures. We know that we are unique creatures, that God has made us in his image, that we have a freedom to do something that nature does not know, that we can project goals beyond the limitations, ambitions, desires, and lusts of nature. We are the creatures who, gloriously, tragically, and pathetically, make history. As we make it, we have to make distinctions between good and evil. We know that selfishness is dangerous. We must be unselfish. The more we rise above our immediate situation and see the situation of the other person, the more creative we are. Therefore, our life story is concerned with making rigorous distinctions between right and wrong, between good and evil. Part of the Christian faith corresponds to this interpretation. Certainly a part of the Old Testament is not quite sure whether man is in relationship to God, or whether the primary job for the righteous is to war against the unrighteous. We have to admit that it makes a very big difference when we defend freedom against tyranny, and truth against the lies of the world. How else could we build history except by these rigorous distinctions between good and evil, right and wrong?

But now we come to the New Testament lesson, the puzzling lesson of the parable of the wheat and the tares. The man sowed a field of wheat and the enemy sowed tares among the wheat. And the servants, following the impulse of each one of us, asked if they should root out the tares so that the wheat could grow. This is a parable taken from agriculture to illustrate a point of morals, and it violates every principle of agriculture or of morals. After all every farmer and every gardener makes ceaseless war against the tares. How else could the flowers and the wheat grow? And we have to make ceaseless war against evil within ourselves and in our fellowmen, or how could there be any kind of decency in the world? Against all moral impulse, we have this eschatological parable.

"Nay," said the householder. "Lest while ye gather up the tares, you root up also the wheat." The suggestion is that a great deal of evil may come from the selfishness of men, but perhaps more evil may come from the premature judgments of men about themselves and each other. "Let both grow together until the harvest." These wonderful words of Scripture suggest that while we have to judge, there is a judgment beyond our judgment, and there are fulfillments beyond our fulfillments.

Consider how much more evil and good, creativity and selfishness, are mixed up in actual life than our moralists, whether they be Christian or secular, realize. How little we achieve charity because we do not recognize this fact.

Let us consider the matter of creativity and the desire for approval. What could be more evil than the avaricious desire for the approval of our fellowmen? But how closely related it is to the impulse of creativity. The diary of Virginia Woolf notes that when she put out a new novel, she had an almost morbid interest in the reviews. She was an established artist. Was her anxiety justified? Could not she just take for granted that people would praise her or would accept her work? Yet she had a morbid concern, as anyone who has written a book understands. You may think that you are creative, but you suspect you may have slipped. You have to be approved in order to establish your creativity; the wheat and the tares are very mixed up. "Let both grow together until the harvest." When we think of ourselves, we ought to remember that there is an ultimate judgment against excessive self-concern. But when we deal with our fellowman, we must do so in charity.

How curiously are love and self-love mixed up in life, much more complexly than any scheme of morals recognizes. The simple words of the parable are more profound than the wisdom of all our moralists.

There is a self-love which is the engine of creativity. It may not be justified ultimately for that reason, but when we look at history, we have to say that it is an engine of creativity.

There is a debate whether Cervantes wrote the great classic, *Don Quixote,* in order to pay his debts, or in order to get even with his critics. But now it does not make any difference what the motive was. *Don Quixote* is no less a great work of art.

In the field of politics we see very clearly the curious mixture of egotism and desire for public welfare. Winston Churchill, for example, was a very ambitious young man. His ambition gave him the chance to accomplish much. What he achieved was not only great statesmanship but had a quality of magnanimity that reminds us of the wisdom of the wheat and the tares. Churchill knew the mixture of good and evil in the dramas of history. We doubt whether he ever read or really heeded the parable of the wheat and the tares, yet in his magnanimity there was some of its wisdom. He showed the combination of creativity and self-love which we find particularly in politics, but is it not everywhere? There is a puzzling aspect to judgments about self-love or ambition. At what particular point do we think egotism so excessive that it becomes obviously corrupting? It is always rather corrupting, but when does it become *obviously* corrupting? We know certain people to be monstrous egotists, but can we put our finger on the spot where this mixture of love and self-love, which we all have, turns into monstrous egotism? We do have to make our judgments, but we cannot be exact in our moral measurement.

There are forms of self-love which are quite dangerous, but are enclosed in a great sea of vitality which robs them of some of their power. Let us compare America with Spain. In Spain, the somewhat medieval social and political order is according to the tradition of natural law and of the Catholic church. To us, it is stale and static. In this country, and in spite of all our weaknesses, our pride and pretensions, certainly there is life. Our national life is based upon the vitality of various interests balanced by various other interests. This is the heart of the free enterprise doctrine. These self-interests are not nearly as harmless as our conservative friends imagine them to be. Here we do have to violate the parable, and provisionally make judgments and say, "This form of self-interest must be checked." Or, "This form of self-interest must be balanced by other interest." Otherwise we will not have justice if the powerful man simply goes after his interest at the expense of the weak.

We make such provisional judgments, but all these provisional judgments stand ultimately under the truth of the parable of the wheat and the tares. "Let both grow together until the harvest." If we had more modesty about this, perhaps there would not have been such a debate between pure individualism and pure collectivism. On the one hand, this policy may be necessary. On the other hand, it may be dangerous. We had better try to find out how necessary and how dangerous it is, but not absolutely, or we will make the kind of judgment that will pull up the wheat with the tares.

What is Communism but a vast example of pulling up the tares, and not knowing the wheat that is among these tares of so called self-interest or capitalistic injustice. Is it not surprising that we should have two great evils in our time, Nazism and Communism? Nazism represented such an obvious expression of collective egotism that we do not have to wait for the ultimate judgment. We all know that Nazism was evil! But Communism is a form of evil that comes from human beings forgetting that they are creatures, imagining themselves omniscient and righteous—absolutely righteous—and trying to rebuild the whole world in terms of their ideals, not knowing that their own sins are involved in it. The Communist knows nothing about the parable of the wheat and the tares, or about the ultimate judgment that stands over human existence, and above all nothing about the ambiguity of all human motives.

There is also that kind of selfishness which we might regard as an inadvertent and rather harmless corruption of the love impulse. Is it really inadvertent? Is it actually harmless? We do not know exactly. The sinfulness of parents in their love for their children gives us an example.

The love of parents for their children is one of the symbols of the kingdom of God. But we parents are not quite perfect. There are two crises which children face: one is in their youth when they find out that their parents are not as powerful as they thought; and the second is in their adolescence when they find out that the parents are not as good as they thought they were. No doubt every parent is better than an adolescent rebel imagines in the period of rebellion. The parent who claims to be absolutely loving and then insinuates into that love the old lust for power, which every human being has, obviously is vexatious. But it also must be recognized that there is some good in this evil.

Thus human history is a mixture of wheat and tares. We must make provisional distinctions, but we must know that there are no final distinctions. "Let both grow together until the harvest." Man is a creature and a creator. He would not be a creator if he could not overlook the human scene and be able to establish goals beyond those of nature and to discriminate between good and evil. He must do these things. But he must also remember that no matter how high his creativity may rise, he is himself involved in the flow of time, and he becomes evil at the precise point where he pretends not to be, when he pretends that his wisdom is not finite but infinite, and his virtue is not ambiguous but unambiguous.

From the standpoint of the biblical faith we do not have to despair because life is so brief, but we must not pretend to more because we are so great. Because we are both small and great, we have discerned a mystery and a meaning beyond our smallness and our greatness, and a justice and a love which completes our incompletions, which corrects our judgments, and which brings the whole story to a fulfillment beyond our power to fulfill any story.

We thank you, our God, for your judgments which are sterner than the judgments of man. Help us to remember them when moral men speak well of us. We thank you for your mercy which is kinder than the goodness of men. Help us to discern this when we are overcome by the confusion of life, and despair about our own sin. Grant us, O Lord, always to worship you in all our doings in the greatness of your creativity and the wonder of your judgment and your mercy.

8.   Beware of Covetousness

All who make idols are nothing, and the things they delight in do not profit; their witnesses neither see nor know, that they may be put to shame. Who fashions a god or casts an image, that is profitable for nothing? Behold, all his fellows shall be put to shame, and the craftsmen are but men; let them all assemble, let them stand forth, they shall be terrified, they shall be put to shame together.

The ironsmith fashions it and works it over the coals; he shapes it with hammers, and forges it with his strong arm; he becomes hungry and his strength fails, he drinks no water and is faint. The carpenter stretches a line, he marks it out with a pencil; he fashions it with planes, and marks it with a compass; he shapes it into the figure of a man, with the beauty of a man, to dwell in a house. He cuts down cedars; or he chooses a holm tree or an oak and lets it grow strong among the trees of the forest; he plants a cedar and the rain nourishes it. Then it becomes fuel for a man; he takes a part of it and warms himself, he kindles a fire and bakes bread; also he makes a god and worships it, he makes it a graven image and falls down before it. Half of it he burns in the fire; over the half he eats flesh, he roasts meat and is satisfied; also he warms himself and says, "Aha, I am warm, I have seen the fire!" And the rest of it he makes into a god, his idol; and falls down to it and worships it; he prays to it and says, "Deliver me, for thou art my god!"

They know not, nor do they discern; for he has shut their eyes, so that they cannot see, and their minds, so that they cannot understand. No

Union Theological Seminary, New York, May 7, 1961.

one considers, nor is there knowledge or discernment to say, "Half of it I burned in the fire, I also baked bread on its coals, I roasted flesh and have eaten; and shall I make the residue of it an abomination? Shall I fall down before a block of wood?" He feeds on ashes; a deluded mind has led him astray, and he cannot deliver himself or say, "Is there not a lie in my right hand?"

Isaiah 44:9–20, RSV

One of the multitude said to him, "Teacher, bid my brother divide the inheritance with me." But he said to him, "Man, who made me a judge or divider over you?" And he said to them, "Take heed, and beware of all covetousness; for a man's life does not consist in the abundance of his possessions." And he told them a parable, saying, "The land of a rich man brought forth plentifully; and he thought to himself, 'What shall I do, for I have nowhere to store my crops?' And he said, 'I will do this: I will pull down my barns, and build larger ones; and there I will store all my grain and my goods. And I will say to my soul, Soul, you have ample goods laid up for many years; take your ease, eat, drink, be merry.' But God said to him, 'Fool! This night your soul is required of you; and the things you have prepared, whose will they be?' So is he who lays up treasure for himself, and is not rich toward God."

Luke 12:13–21, RSV

The statement that a man's life does not consist in the abundance of his possessions is unassailable. The warning, therefore, to "take heed and beware of all covetousness" is certainly valid, yet we violate it. Why do we? For a good and bad reason; or, perhaps not for a good reason, rather, for an inevitable reason. The inevitable and the sinful reason that we violate it is that all of the desires of man are indeterminate. He has no simple *terminus ad quem* for any of his desires; so he desires more than he needs, and this is sinful. But the good reason is that these desires for the abundance of goods are inextricably mixed up with all the creative capacities of man. That is why we cannot follow our Lord's warning without a great deal of thought and discrimination. This is one of the many passages of scripture where the Church can be relevant today only if it accepts the ultimate truth of the gospel, and then applies it to our life with discrimination. Let us look at these things against which our Lord warns us.

We *have* to have things because we need, as do the animals, food and shelter. We have more things than do the animals not just because we need them, but because we are intelligent. We have more food and shelter than the animals because we have foresight and a good deal of dexterity in building our shelters which they do not have. We have hands and they have only feet. An interesting thing about clothing is that it also belongs to "things." We cover our nakedness against the winter's cold with clothing. Have you ever wondered about this aspect of the evolutionary process? Did we become intelligent because we were naked, and so had to get the fur of other animals to cover us; or did God in the evolutionary process anticipate our intelligence and make us naked, knowing that we would use the skins of other animals to cover us?

We have food, shelter, clothing—but more than these—tools. Tools belong to the abundance of things. What are tools but the symbols of our creativity? Karl Marx said that man is *homo faber,* the maker of tools. But this is not quite true, for man's spirituality and intellectuality make him more than a tool-making animal. What are these tools —these wheels that are in many respects more efficient than our legs —but extensions of our physical capacities? Telescopes and microscopes are extensions of our eyes. Telephones are extensions of our ears. Other tools are the more dexterous and powerful fingers of our hands. Terrible nuclear weapons can be seen as awful extensions of our fists. What a marvelous and yet a terrible thing is this creativity of man; but note how the abundance of things is mixed up with his creativity. We have things because we need them. We have things because we are human and we can make them. But that is not all, and that is why Jesus warns us, "Take heed, and beware of all covetousness," for there is another aspect of this to examine.

Inevitably we worship the things that are meant as means. Such is the freedom of man that we cannot keep all this in order. We worship the things that ought to be means, and we make them ends in themselves, indeed we make them God.

The prophet Isaiah was speaking against primitive idolatry in our first Scripture lesson. Isaiah said, you grow a tree, the carpenters plane it, you use the powder to bake bread, to roast meat, and to warm yourself, and you forget that you have warmed yourself, that you have planed this tree; yet the residue you make into a god as a totem pole. Now that is primitive idolatry. People may say, "Of course, but that is not relevant to *our* life." But the fact of idolatry is relevant, for we all are inclined to make things into ends rather than means, and ultimate ends, that is, gods. "A man's life does not consist in the abundance of his possessions." Life consists in self-fulfillment, and self-fulfillment is not possible without using self, or subordinating self to a more ultimate purpose and will than our will. This is the whole point of the hierarchy of values in which we live. For things are complicated, and in the creativities we have to be discriminate, but when we talk about discrimination we do not know where to draw the line.

We know that we are living in a so-called economy of abundance. Most of us do not eat more food than we ought to except on ritual occasions. As for clothing, that is a difficult thing, because we certainly have more clothing than is necessary to keep out the winter's cold. Academic gowns, for example, are not for that purpose. They are partly symbolic and partly the instruments of pride. Who can deny that? My academic gown shows that I am a professor. Professors in academic processions may be preening their feathers of academic honors. If they are theological professors, perhaps they will preach sermons the following Sunday, as I used to, about women who wear mink stoles. Mink stoles may not have the same kind of symbolic utility as has the academic gown. But does not that show that even our drawing of lines is ideologically tainted? And our clothing likewise?

Who would deny that our houses express symbolically how important we are in the community? Or they may be a necessity of our function in the community. When a Vice President suddenly becomes President, within twenty-four hours he has to move into the White House, because the pressure of business and the symbolic nature of the presidential office make it necessary for him to be in the White House. These things cannot be called simply "good" or "bad," for they are not only the tools of our physical life, but the tools of our culture and extensions of ourselves.

Likewise, there are the instruments of music, the tools of our art, where the wings of our imagination reach to heaven. Also the tools of our science, the laboratories and the doctor's scalpel, and so forth. A radical asceticism which runs all through religious history from the prophet Amos to Francis of Assisi cuts the line too sharply and excludes the instruments of culture. "They," says the prophet Amos talking about the rich people, "make themselves instruments of music like David. They shouldn't do that." The relationship of culture to privilege is very bothersome. There was some years ago a professor of Christian ethics who said, "Let us put a moratorium on all art and science until we have solved the problem of justice." But can we do that?

A rich young man asked Jesus, "Master, what good deed must I do to have eternal life?" and Jesus answered, "Keep the commandments." The young man said, "All these I have observed. What do I still lack?" "If you would be perfect," which means—oh, well, you want something more than that—"go sell what you possess, and give to the poor." What is important here is the command, "give to the poor." This we will consider later.

St. Francis of Assisi was asked by one of his friars, "Brother Francis, couldn't I have a Bible of my own even if I'm wedded to Lady Poverty?" And Francis said, "If I give you a Bible, you'll ask for a breviary, and if I give you a breviary, you'll soon have a whole library." So the friar did not have the Bible or the breviary or the library. But a century after Francis, the Franciscan order took over the University of Paris and founded the University of Oxford. This development may be in violation of the gospel story about the rich young man, but it is according to the facts of life.

There is a radical tendency in religion which is so worried about the inordinance of human desires that it wants to cut out all desires, forgetting that we face always and everywhere a mixture of creative and inordinate desires. Today we face this problem in a particular way in a so-called economy of abundance. Ever since the Industrial Revolution we have had a great temptation to worship things: automobiles, television, et cetera. Are these things our luxuries or necessities? Will we begrudge our middle-class families their model kitchens? All we can say is that they ought not to have a religious reverence for their kitchens or their automobiles. The religious overtone is what is wrong. A European professor who came here years ago said, "I'm surprised that all the American parsons I've met have bigger automobiles than libraries." This is the temptation of a great, wealthy nation, the temptation of inordinance in the worship of things. And yet we cannot say simply, "Let us get rid of these things," because at some level or other —we have to try to find where is that level—these things are related to our creativities, and ultimately to the life of the spirit. The instruments of music that Amos wanted to get rid of, and the libraries that Francis of Assisi wanted to get rid of are tools of the spirit.

The real problem is not how much or how little we possess, but the number of things, or advantages and security for our family, that we have over against what our brother has.

Let us take this in two categories, the so-called class struggle within the nations, and the natural struggle between the have and the have-not nations. All through the history of civilizations things have multiplied as culture has grown. The cultures of ancient Egypt and Samaria multiplied things as the culture became more advanced. The Romans had their wonderful baths, but the Romans had a culture superior to the barbarians of the European continent. The interesting thing about this multiplication of things, and the multiplication of culture, was that it was always at the price of human brotherhood. It was always at the price of injustice. Because as these cities grew, the old brotherhood disappeared, and the rich became richer and the poor became poorer. Finally when we reached the climax of civilization—climax, that is, only in technical terms—the Industrial Revolution of the nineteenth century, it seemed for a moment that these disparities of injustice were aggravated beyond endurance. That is also how Communism got into the world.

It is interesting that we have been relatively immune from Communism in the Western world. The democratic states of the West devised schemes to get a rough balance of power within the industrial system which made it possible for people to live with one another without unduly resenting each other. This achievement was mostly, but not wholly, by the providence of God and the inadvertence of history rather than by any virtue of man. The rich people and the powerful people resisted all these tendencies until they could not resist them any more. After we had established this tolerable brotherhood, not only in America but in our whole Western civilization, then the new dimension of abundance came upon us. How shrewdly the Communists have taken advantage of not only the class struggle, but the national struggle between the poorest nations and the rich nations. And here we are, the USA, the richest of all the nations.

This social problem is the result of an abundance of things. But we cannot say simply, "Oh yes, it is a problem. Let us share. . . . Let us share." The church is sentimental when it simply says, "Let us share." We're not good enough to share. We're not good enough to say to

India, for example, "Let us equalize our wealth with your poverty." We're not good enough to say that to one African state in need. We have standards twice as high as many parts of Europe, many more times as high as those in other parts of the world. What we have to realize is that wealth and poverty are on the whole not due to exploitation, although there is always exploitation of the weak by the strong. It is a matter of technical competence. The rich nations on the whole are the technically competent nations, and the poor nations are the technically incompetent nations. We are not good enough to share everything that comes out of technical competence, but we must be good enough and wise enough to share the competence, the skill by which the abundance of things can be produced or created.

This is the ethical problem, the ultimate religious problem turned into the ethical terms of a technical society. Much of Christian teaching down the ages has been in terms of serving or saving the soul, but not the body. But man, as society, exists as soul in a body. What we do in the body affects the attitudes of the soul. Despite the question asked in Shakespeare's sonnet,

> Poor soul, why dost thou pine within, and suffer dearth
> Painting thy outward walls so costly gay?
> Why so great a cost, having so short a thrift,
> Dost thou upon thy fading mansions spend?

and the wonderful climax, "So shalt thou feed on Death, that feeds on men," we must search for other ways both to ask questions and to search for proximate solutions to the technical problems of goods in our contemporary world.

St. Luke's Gospel concludes the story from which our text is taken with the parable of the rich fool.

And he told them a parable, saying, "The land of a rich man brought forth plentifully; and he thought to himself, 'What shall

I do, for I have nowhere to store my crops?' And he said, 'I will do this: I will pull down my barns, and build larger ones; and there I will store all my grain and my goods. And I will say to my soul, Soul, you have ample goods laid up for many years; take your ease, eat, drink, be merry.' But God said to him, 'Fool! This night your soul is required of you; and the things you have prepared, whose will they be?' So is he who lays up treasure for himself, and is not rich toward God."

This parable perhaps expresses our problem better than do the words of Shakespeare, which is to witness to our Christian faith in a technical civilization. Let us try to be "rich toward God" rather than lay up treasure for ourselves.

We thank you, our Father that you have made us creators together with you. We thank you that you have given us all the creative abilities to master nature and subordinate her to our purposes. Save us from the folly of believing that we need not subordinate our purposes to your purposes. Save us from the folly of all idolatry and inordinate desires.

9. Intercession

O God, who made your people a royal priesthood that they might offer intercession and prayer for all men, hear us as we pray:

For all who toil in the burden and heat of the day in forest and farm, in mine and factory, on land and sea, that they may enjoy the fruits of their industry, that they may not be defrauded of their rightful due, and that we may never cease to be mindful of our debt to them, remembering with gratitude the multitude of services which must be performed to make our life tolerable.

For all those who have authority over their fellowmen, that they may never use it selfishly for themselves, their party, or their class, but may be guided to do justice and to love mercy and to walk humbly, remembering whose servants they are.

For those who have been worsted in the struggle of life, whether by the inhumanity of their fellows, their own limitations, or by those hazards of life which beset all men, that they may contend against injustice without bitterness, overcome their own weakness with diligence, and learn to accept with patience that which cannot be altered.

For the rulers of the nations, that they may act wisely and without pride, seeking always to promote peace among the peoples and establish justice in our common life.

∽∾∾

Look with pity, our Father, upon the world in its sorrow, and upon the sighing of your children, for we are engulfed by the evil of our own contriving. May those who suffer because they are guilty, learn the godly sorrow of true repentance. May those who suffer innocently have a vision of the suffering of Christ, and know that there is redemption in their pain. If we have mediated your wrath to the guilty, help us also to be instruments of your mercy to them. If the innocent sufferers of the world have brought the knowledge of mercy to us, help us now to be servants of your love toward them, binding up their wounds, stilling their hunger, and restoring them to home and family. Grant, O Lord, that through your grace, the world which glorifies itself may die, and a new world may be born which gives you the glory, through Jesus Christ Our Lord.

O God, before whom to bow is to stand truly, and whom to know is to know ourselves in what we are and what we ought to be, save us from all vain pretensions about ourselves, so that under your judgment and by your mercy we may find ourselves.

Let us pray for all who are in special need of God's grace:

O Lord, we commend to your mercy all who are in anxiety or distress, most particularly the hungry multitudes of Asia and Africa, who suffer from the want of their daily bread. Enlarge our hearts toward them, that we may not perish in surfeit while they perish in hunger.

We pray also for those who suffer from the cruelty and contempt of arrogant men and nations. Grant them the inner dignity and hope which is able to defy the neglect and contempt of their fellows.

We pray for all men in authority in industry and government, upon whose decisions hang the welfare of their fellows. Give them the humility to see that their strength is not their own but is of the community they serve. Make them wise in this humility so that they may not be tempted to any unjust or foolish action by pride or vainglory.

O Lord, give us all the grace to serve thee in our several callings and to minister to our fellowmen the more charitably because we walk humbly before our God.

Grant us grace, O Lord, to learn of your judgments which overtake us when we set brother against brother and nation against nation; give us wisdom and strength to fashion better instruments for our common life, so that we may dwell in concord under your providence. May your kingdom come among us through Jesus Christ our Lord.

O Lord, who has set us in a day of great confusion and of great hope, you have tried us by many perplexities and disciplined us with many responsibilities. Help us to live in the trials of our day with patience and to meet our tasks with courage. When the confusion of claims threatens to overwhelm us, guide us by your grace; when our tasks are beyond our powers, assist us with your power; when our own fears and ambitions add to the world's woes, overrule us so that despite our weakness your will may be done.

We pray, O Lord, for your children everywhere, for those who are in great distress and in pain of body or soul by reason of the tumults of this age, the cruelties of men, and the indifference of their fellows. We pray for all those who have suffered and now suffer and are destitute, afflicted, or tormented. And grant that our hearts may go out to their needs, so that we may become vehicles of your mercy to them.

We pray for all rulers and men of authority in all nations, and for all who have power over their fellowmen, and who make decisions upon which the weal and woe of nations depend. Teach them the wisdom which is drawn from true humility. Let their hearts be filled with the fear of God, so that they will not use their power wrongfully. Give all little men and judges and presidents and commissars, who are great beyond their strength, by reason of the strength which they have drawn from and owe to the community, a sense of that judgment which stands against the judges of the earth, and which renders their counsels vain when directed against the counsels of God.

O God, who taught us to pray for the coming of your kingdom on this earth, give us grace to build our communities after the fashion of your kingdom, to set no boundaries about them which you would not set, to quiet the tumult and strife within them by brotherly love, and to work the more diligently for concord within them, because our final hope is in the city which has foundations, whose builder and maker is God.

⇛❦⇝

O Lord, good shepherd of the sheep, who wills not that any should perish, but that all men should be saved and come to the knowledge of your truth, give grace to those who seek your lost sheep in the wilderness of this world's corruption.

⇛❦⇝

Hear us, our Father, as we pray for all who are in special need of your grace; for the sick and the anxious; for the dying and those who stand in the fear of death. Teach them that neither life nor death can separate them from the love of God.

We pray for those who have great authority that they may know the limits of human wisdom, and may seek your counsels to supply their need. We pray for doctors and nurses and all who are ministers of your mercy, that they may be fit vehicles of your grace, and for all teachers and guides of youth that they may rightly divide the word of truth and lead men to wisdom and to the fear of the Lord which is the beginning of wisdom.

Finally, we pray for ourselves that our conscience may be stirred by your word and that our anxieties may be quieted by your love, so that we may do our work and meet our duties with the peace which comes not from our goodness but from your grace.

We bring before you, O Lord, the needs of all your children. Help us to remember with concern the multitudes whom you love more than we can, and for whom we would pray, as your love for them reaches our hearts. Help us to remember the sorrowing and the sighing of all who suffer at the hands of their fellowmen: the hunted and the persecuted, the miserable and forsaken, the homeless and wandering. O Lord, save your people and have pity upon all of us for the great confusion of the nations. Hasten the day when they will find order and peace for their common life.

O God, in whom there is no darkness at all, we thank you that though we walk in darkness, you have given us enough light in which to walk. As the sun dispels each morning the shadows of the night, so your mercies, which surround us, pierce the shadows of sin ever and again, and help us to see the meaning of our life. Give us grace to triumph over the confusion of impulse, in which we are so easily ensnared, and to walk in the way disclosed by your wisdom. Grant us clearness of vision especially when good is intertwined with evil, and when duty conflicts with desire, so that we may do your will this day and always.

O God, whom the heavens cannot contain, yet who visits the humble with your presence, and loves a contrite heart, give us eyes to see our share in the common sins of mankind, so that we will not walk in pride and deceive ourselves. In all our doings, reveal yourself to us, a God both of wrath and mercy, who visits the sins of the fathers upon the children to the third and fourth generation and who shows mercy to them that love you. We are consumed by your anger and sustained by your mercy. Such knowledge is too wonderful for us. We cannot attain to it. Yet we know that in an evil world we are sustained by your grace coming to us in the goodness of generous souls, in forgiving hearts, in the beneficences of nature, of the glory of the day, the rhythm of the seasons, and in the whole solemn mystery of life. Make us more worthy of the swift and solemn trust of life.

O Lord, show yourself to all who seek you, give peace to all who are anxious and afraid, and challenge all the strong and the secure that they may know their strength is not their own, and that they are not as secure as they think they are.

We pray, O Lord, for the millions of distressed people throughout the earth.

May our hearts go out to them, and grant that we may become the ministers of your mercy to them, more especially since they bear in their bodies the costly price of our freedom and security.

10. Be Not Anxious

"Do not store up for yourselves treasure on earth, where it grows rusty and moth-eaten, and thieves break in to steal it. Store up treasure in heaven, where there is no moth and no rust to spoil it, no thieves to break in and steal. For where your treasure is, there will your heart be also.

"The lamp of the body is the eye. If your eyes are sound, you will have light for your whole body; if the eyes are bad, your whole body will be in darkness. If then the only light you have is darkness, the darkness is doubly dark.

"No servant can be the slave of two masters; for either he will hate the first and love the second, or he will be devoted to the first and think nothing of the second. You cannot serve God and Money.

"Therefore I bid you put away anxious thoughts about food and drink to keep you alive, and clothes to cover your body. Surely life is more than food, the body more than clothes. Look at the birds of the air; they do not sow and reap and store in barns, yet your heavenly Father feeds them. You are worth more than the birds! Is there a man of you who by anxious thought can add a foot to his height? And why be anxious about clothes? Consider how the lilies grow in the fields; they do not work, they do not spin; and yet, I tell you, even Solomon in all his splendour was not attired like one of these. But if that is how God clothes the grass in the fields, which is there today, and tomorrow is thrown on the stove, will he not all the more clothe you? How little faith you have! No, do not ask anxiously, 'What are we to eat? What are we to drink? What shall we wear?' All these are things for the heathen to

Memorial Church, Harvard University, October 22, 1961.

*run after, not for you, because your heavenly Father knows that you
need them all. Set your mind on God's kingdom and his justice before
everything else, and all the rest will come to you as well. So do not be
anxious about tomorrow; tomorrow will look after itself. Each day has
troubles enough of its own."*

Matthew 6:19–34, NEB

Two points are significant about this text with its warning against
preoccupation with the future and its affirmation about the significance of the present. One is that it is very uncharacteristic both of
biblical faith and of Western civilization. The second is that it is very
relevant for a nuclear age, precisely because it is uncharacteristic.

Biblical faith in both the Old and the New Testaments laid the
foundation for the historical dynamism of the West by the hazardous
affirmation that human history is meaningful. This affirmation involved Messianic hopes, either as consequence or as presupposition,
positing a Messianic age in which all the meaninglessness and the
cross-purposes of history would be resolved under a divine Messianic
ruler.

Jesus spent his whole ministry in an atmosphere of Messianic ex-
pectations and speculations. Would the Messiah come? Or, had he
come? Was Jesus himself the Messiah? "Who do men say that I am?"
he asked his disciples. Many passages from the prophet Isaiah illustrate two of the perennial motifs in the Messianic hopes of Hebraic
prophecy. They are archetypal. The one motif is the projection of the
Messianic Davidic king, the Shepherd king, who will bring righteousness and justice, who will gently lead his sheep and carry the lambs
in his bosom. In short, he will combine perfect love with great power.
He thus will resolve the perennial moral ambiguity of all political
systems derived from the fact that power is never perfectly coor-
dinated to the ends of justice. This hope may be naive, but it is really
more profound than modern utopian hopes. These expect rulers to

combine virtue with power, whereas we know with Lord Acton, that "power corrupts and absolute power corrupts absolutely." The Messianic hope of the Old Testament, and even the earlier Egyptian Messianic hope for the Shepherd king, assumed that such a king would and must be a God-king.

The other archetypal theme found in the same prophet is the hope of a transformed nature, which alone would make a redeemed history possible. "The calf and the young lion shall grow up together and a little child shall lead them." This hope expresses the shrewd insight into historical reality, namely, that its cruelties and inhumanities are but accentuations of the cruelties of nature, which is, as we know, red in tooth and claw. Since history is but an elaboration of nature, it is surely more naive and yet profound to assert that history cannot be redeemed unless nature is transformed, than to expect—as all modern utopianism does—the fulfillment of an unconditioned good on the basis of the contingent conditions of nature-history.

The theme "a little child shall lead them" is also archetypal. Hopes of a future ideal age are usually related to a nostalgic estimate of an innocent past which will be restored. This nostalgia in regard to childhood is natural. We are guilty now, but we believe that we were purer when we were children—a fact our parents might dispute. In terms of collective nostalgia every nation seems to have notions of an innocent past. The seventeenth-century English Puritan writers of their Civil War period assumed an innocent past before the Norman conquest. We Americans usually place the period of innocence before our Civil War or before our industrialization. Thus we reenact collectively what we experience individually. Presumably, we were innocent before freedom was fully developed. The "Fall" is curiously related to the growth of freedom. But why should the continued growth of freedom usher in a new age of virtue?

Despite the implausibility of these hopes for the future, it is significant that it was such a dominant theme in Western civilization. Later, when orthodox Christianity was dissolved or diluted by secularism, and when the millennium was transmuted into utopia in the seventeenth century, this theme was not eroded or diluted. It was indeed more firmly established. Everybody believed in progress and in the perfectibility of man. This was the dominant religious belief of both Christians and agnostics.

When I first began my annual visits to Harvard thirty-four years ago, I observed, in commuting between the church and the university, that despite the debate between the religious and the academic community, they were agreed in this implausible hope. The learned community hoped for progress by developing techniques of wider rationality and the religious community hoped for progress through increasing piety.

There were many forms of the idea of progress. Those who followed Spencer and the "social Darwinists" believed that wars were occasioned by the poverty of agricultural societies and would be eliminated by the wealth of industrial civilizations. We might make some ironic reflections about the vanity of this hope by the wisdom of hindsight in a nuclear age.

The idea of progress, derived from the thought of the French sociologist, Auguste Comte, did not make the mistake of equating history with nature. On the contrary, it based its hope on increasing rationality in history and on human power over nature, which ultimately would enable a generation of elite scientists—a novel kind of philosopher-kings—to propel history to "socially" approved goals. Thus history would be transfigured by the genius of man.

Another or third form of Messianism, that of the Communists, need concern us only momentarily. It developed, not on the ground of a progressing bourgeois society, but among the victims of early industrialism. It hoped for the kingdom of perfect justice, not by evolution but by revolution, when the disinterested poor, the "proletariat," the industrial workers, would take the leap which would transform history "from the realm of necessity to the realm of freedom."

But we must observe that when the "poor" are blessed with historical success and acquire the power of a commissar, when a Communist sits on the throne of the Tsars, he does not usher in the kingdom of righteousness but merely presides over a despotism much more dynamic and more creative, but also more dangerous, than that of moribund Tsarism. Evidently history solves no problems without creating new ones.

These preoccupations with the future, these efforts to compensate for the trials of the present by illusions about the future, reigned supreme for three centuries. Then came the wintry twentieth century. The nineteeth century had its effective ending in the First World War in 1914. The tragedy of that war eroded utopianism and messianism in Europe. In America, only touched peripherally by the war, the mood changed in the Great Depression. Woodrow Wilson was in fact the last great messianist with his hope of "making the world safe for democracy."

But the differences between Europe and America were dissolved by subsequent history with the Second World War and the "cold war" between the allied victors over Nazism, and finally the dread nuclear dilemma. Now we are preoccupied by the perils of a nuclear catastrophe, so much so that we have not come to terms with the dimension of the spiritual crisis of our age, occasioned by the fact that we have been robbed of hope that the future will cure the ills of the present. A cynic might observe that we heed the warning against preoccupation with the future only because the future contains a peril of such magnitude that the imagination boggles in seeking to comprehend it.

But this deep spiritual problem remains. The tragic experiences and disillusioned hopes from 1914 on should have taught us that the whole style and stance of Western civilization must change radically and that history itself is not the solution of the problems of history.

Rather, it cumulates and enlarges every problem.

We now know what we should have always known, that technical progress increases the scope of man's power over nature, but that all human power contains potentialities both of creativity and of destructiveness.

In the second place we now know what we should have always known, that progress in human rationality is not absolute. No one would assert that any modern philosopher is "more intelligent" than Aristotle, for instance. There is more diffusion of education, and perhaps an accumulation of wisdom. Yet all the achievements of modern culture, including the disciplined mind and the winged imagination, cannot change the fact that when the self, individual or collective, is "cornered," even the purest mind becomes the servant of the anxious self and is not its master. The persistence of petty jealousies in these great academic centers of intellectual life should have taught us more about this problem.

We are, in short, living in a day in which "things hidden have become revealed." It is therefore a new day culturally and spiritually. The warnings of the text against preoccupation about tomorrow are particularly relevant to this day. We can only live if we seek to solve the immediate problems that confront us, since "every day has troubles enough of its own." Dreaming about tomorrow may be just an evasion of possible immediate duties and opportunities today.

The new generation which has come to power in our nation seems to understand somewhat the necessity of this modesty and moderation. But it is for the generation represented in the pews of this church to develop the posture, the stance, the style adequate for bearing the burdens of this era without illusion or hysteria. A few suggestions about this style may be in order. This generation cannot afford to indulge in the absolutist solutions which were the glory and the illusion of my generation. We cannot indulge the hope of a world government when the immediate problem is how to achieve minimal community with a shrewd and ruthless foe by discerning the common humanity below our enmities and, above all, the common involvement in the predicament of nuclear guilt.

We cannot afford the absolute solutions of yesterday for another reason. We are involved in contradictory responsibilities—the maintenance of peace abroad and the preservation of our liberties at home, for instance. That situation makes vivid the perennial predicament of man's political life, which is to seek for proximate solutions of insoluble problems, especially the problem of realizing partly contradictory and partly complementary ends, such as liberty and equality. If we press for ultimate solutions, we are tempted to evade our immediate problems.

Secondly, it is necessary to emphasize the intrinsic, rather than the instrumental, dimension of any act or policy. There are always these two dimensions, but our preoccupation with the future has obscured the intrinsic dimension. An assistant secretary of state recently warned that there were dangerous tendencies of extreme belligerency or defeatism in our national life. This means that some portions of our nation are not patient enough to achieve the virtue of integrity in the days of pressure. The problems which our nation faces are bound to generate these evasions from integrity. We imagined ourselves an innocent nation (shades of Jefferson and Wilson) and now we are in dread of the proleptic guilt of a nuclear war. We were so much the masters of our destiny in the days of our youthful innocence. Now we are so frustrated in the days of our seeming omnipotence.

There are two obvious dangers in preoccupation with the duties of the present. There is always a danger of irresponsibility when hope is not a simple expectation, and when a generation is robbed of the simple solutions which beguiled my generation. How can we sow when we do not know whether we are promised a rich harvest? How can we store when we do not know whether we have a chance to eat what we store? But this danger of irresponsibility can be partly overcome by a mature reflection that each present is so pregnant with the future that fulfilling present tasks may be more responsible than dreaming about an ideal future. Thus, turning again to the international situation: it is more important to consider the immediate realities of this curious contest and partnership with the Russians than to dream of world government.

It is very speculative that the partnership in responsibility to save the world from nuclear disaster might become ultimately the basis of community. But it is not as speculative as constructing an ideal "Parliament of Mankind and Federation of the World." Immediate prospects can be responsibly exploited, though with less illusion than other generations required to nerve themselves for their tasks. There are organic growths in the historical life of man which must be carefully nursed and tended. The human community on all levels is such an organism. There is some artifact in every community, but the organic aspects of our collective life have been neglected in our preoccupation with the future. It is easier to build a house than to tend a garden and weed it every week. Hence we have emphasized the contrived, rather than the organic, processes in the growth of the community.

The most obvious temptation for a generation living in this wintry era is the temptation to self-pity. It is difficult even to complain, "The time is out of joint. O cursed spite, that ever I was born to set it right." For the path to setting things right is not clear. It is more difficult to rejoice with Rupert Brooke, "God be thanked who has matched us with this hour." But something of that temper must enter our soul. The whole of humanity faces the most difficult trials of human history. We can avoid self-pity by mature reflection on the significance for us of the great problems which historical destiny has deposited on our doorstep.

There is a possible third temptation which hitherto has not been a peril for Western man. That is to use the present moment as a launching pad for a mystical flight from the terrors of history to the peace of eternity. Fortunately, it has been the ineluctable destiny of Western spirituality to accept the trials of historical responsibility. Zen Buddhism may be an option in Japan, and mystical world-flight a possibility in the Orient. But Nirvana is not for us, even if the gates of Utopia have been closed to us. That, incidentally, spells out the whole dimension of our problem.

Human life is historical, and we cannot evade the constitution of our life. We must not be preoccupied about tomorrow, but it is still a fact that tomorrow is the day when the promise of youth is fulfilled. Tomorrow is the day when young love, with its alternations of ecstasy and romantic anxieties, is fulfilled in the blessed stability of a marriage partnership. Tomorrow, of course, is also the day when death and decay impend, as those of us are aware who have passed the meridian of life. Tomorrow fulfills all things and destroys all things and creates new problems while it solves old ones. We always should have known that the mysteries of history do not solve the mysteries of human existence. They are another dimension of that mystery. Now we know it beyond peradventure of doubt. The current generation must come to terms with this fact and develop trust and patience congruent with it.

O Lord, who holds all our yesterdays, todays, and tomorrows in your eternal presence, we thank you that in imagination and reason we are fearfully and wonderfully made, transcending time and thus becoming creators with you. Give us grace to know we do not share your foresight into the future or your power over it. So may we humbly ransom our own time because our days are evil.

11. The Son of Man Must Suffer

> Rejoice greatly, O daughter of Zion!
>> Shout aloud, O daughter of Jerusalem!
> Lo, your king comes to you;
>> triumphant and victorious is he,
> humble and riding on an ass,
>> on a colt the foal of an ass.
>
> *Zechariah 9:9, RSV*

And when they drew near to Jerusalem and came to Bethphage, to the Mount of Olives, then Jesus sent two disciples, saying to them, "Go into the village opposite you, and immediately you will find an ass tied, and a colt with her; untie them and bring them to me. If any one says anything to you, you shall say, 'The Lord has need of them,' and he will send them immediately." This took place to fulfil what was spoken by the prophet, saying,

> "Tell the daughter of Zion,
> Behold, your king is coming to you,
> humble, and mounted on an ass,
> and on a colt, the foal of an ass."

The disciples went and did as Jesus had directed them; they brought the ass and the colt, and put their garments on them, and he sat thereon. Most of the crowd spread their garments on the road, and others cut branches from the trees and spread them on the road. And

Memorial Church, Harvard University, Palm Sunday, April 15, 1962.

the crowds that went before him and that followed him shouted,
"Hosanna to the Son of David! Blessed be he who comes in the name
of the Lord! Hosanna in the highest!" And when he entered Jerusalem,
all the city was stirred, saying, "Who is this?" And the crowds said,
"This is the prophet Jesus from Nazareth of Galilee."

Matthew 21:1–11, RSV

On the first day of the week they hailed him as a triumphant
Messiah with loud hosannahs. Our Palm Sunday is a liturgical re-
enactment of this triumphal entry into Jerusalem, riding on "an ass
and the colt of an ass" as the ancient prophet had predicted. On the
fifth day of the week they (that is, another "they" of enemies) cried
"crucify him" and a reluctant Roman governor, Pontius Pilate, condemned him to death on the cross. In between these two events were
all the historical incidents, the observance of the Last Supper, the
agony in the Garden of Gethsemane, the betrayal of Peter and the
greater betrayal of another disciple, Judas, which are enacted liturgi-
cally in Holy Week.

The crowd which hailed him as a triumphant Messiah probably
consisted of sympathizers, rather than disciples. They did not know,
in any event, that Jesus had himself renounced the role of a triumphant Messiah who would bring victory to the righteous over the
unrighteous, and had chosen instead the role of a suffering servant,
as suggested by the prophecies in the writings of Isaiah. He had
predicted his own death and insisted that the Son of Man had come
"not to be served but to serve, and to give his life as a ransom for
many."

The difference in those five days of Holy Week represents the
difference between the old and new Hebraic religions. They are both
creative in making the hazardous assertion that the drama of human
history has meaning. The old religion tried to solve the problem of the
moral ambiguity of the historical process by projecting a Messianic

age in which all ambiguity would be eliminated by the triumph of justice over injustice. The new religion, despite the idea of a suffering Messiah rather than a triumphant one, also had many Messianic moods and movements.

It is difficult to renounce the idea that the mixtures of good and evil in men and nations, which give the drama of history such pathos and an infinite variety of themes, will be eliminated by a final triumph of good over evil; even though the clear meaning of the suffering servant, as Jesus interpreted it, was that history reached its climax of meaning, not in the triumph of good over evil, but in the contrite awareness that all men, good and evil, must be reconciled to God.

Let us not observe Palm Sunday by a polemical attitude toward the old Messianism, and a congratulation for Christians that Christianity is superior to Judaism. The distinguished Jewish philosopher, Martin Buber, accurately defined the differences between the two religions in this way: "To the Christian, the Jew is a stubborn fellow, who in an unredeemed world still is waiting for the Messiah. To the Jew, the Christian is the heedless fellow who, in an unredeemed world, affirms that redemption has somehow or other taken place."

Since the ethical impulses of the Christian faith are inherited from the Jewish faith, with its sense of justice, with its law of love, with its emphasis on historical responsibility, it is not our business to convert Jews to Christianity. It is more important that each individual make the most creative use of the framework of meaning that each faith constructs for the faithful, than that we should engage in polemical attitudes about the real or supposed superiorities in the competitive frames of meaning. Let us leave with the Jews the problem of what it means to be "still waiting for the Messiah"; and whether, translated in modern terms, this could mean any more than a perennial utopianism, which has played such a creative but also confusing role in the history of mankind. Let Christians be concerned with their own problem, as expressed in Buber's phrase: "The Christian is a heedless fellow, who affirms, that in an unredeemed world, redemption has somehow or other taken place."

That "somehow or other" is obviously related to the death of Christ on the cross. This symbol has had a mysterious power in all the ages of Christianity. It evidently touches deep springs of mystery and meaning in the life of mankind. It might be profitable to explore two partly complementary and partly contradictory interpretations of that "somehow or other" of the story of the cross in Western Christian culture. On the one hand, the death on the cross means an heroic effort of self-regarding men, whose inveterate self-love is the root of all historical evil, to transmute self-regard into self-forgetfulness, into "sacrificial love" or love of the neighbor. This interpretation is rooted in Christ's own words, "If anyone wishes to be a follower of mine, he must leave self behind, he must take up his cross and come with me"; or in the exhortation: "There must be no limit to your goodness, as your heavenly Father's goodness knows no bounds." It is expressed by Paul: "Have that bearing toward one another which also was found in Christ Jesus . . . who assuming the nature of a slave . . . in obedience accepted even death on a cross." It is also expressed in all the ethical teachings, of which the Sermon on the Mount is an example, which challenge the Christian disciple to a conduct heedless of any self-interest.

On the other hand, the cross is a symbol of a quite different meaning. It emphasizes that the life of good and evil men is inextricably involved in a mixture of noble and petty impulses, of concern for the self and concern for the other, and that this mixture of good and evil cannot be overcome by taking thought, or by one more heroic effort to secure the triumph of good over evil; but that mankind must look at the cross of Christ, not as the triumph in defeat of a noble man, but as a symbol of the merciful action of a forgiving God, "who knows our frame and remembers that we are dust." Jesus expressed this meaning in his interpretation of his Messianic mission: he spoke of the

Son of Man who "did not come to be served, but to give his life as a ransom for many." Paul, as usual, expressed the theme in a grand religious symbol: "God was in Christ, reconciling the world to himself." The thesis on which the Christian faith was founded was that this reconciliation between all men and God had taken place in the suffering and death of the Messiah; and that this event challenged good and evil men to become aware in contrition of the variance between their mixed motives and the ultimate demands of love. They could be charitable and compassionate toward their fellows only against the background of a faith which knew, in the words of the priest in Shorthouse's "John Inglesant," that "only the infinite pity is adequate for the infinite pathos of human existence."

This second theme, elaborated in Christian faith from the events of Holy Week, is much more in accord with the facts of human existence, for it challenges us to a modest self-awareness of the bewildering mixture of good and evil in every human heart. Perhaps it is more creative of compassion than heroic efforts at self-sacrifice. Yet men, though inveterately self-regarding, still have an uneasy conscience by what Pascal terms the self's "perverse desire for height," so that the cross as a symbol of heroic self-giving is a frame of meaning for all noble acts of life, in which the tyranny of the self over the self is transcended: the mother's love, the martyr's sacrifice, the soldier's death for his community, and, indeed, all acts of grace and concern by gracious people for the weal of their neighbors.

This first theme of the climax in the Christ drama, which furnishes the arch for the frame of meaning in the Christian interpretation of human existence, undoubtedly will stand. It also has been the occasion for many abortive attempts to give redemption in an unredeemed world a strenuous moral meaning by efforts of calculated forms of "selflessness." These attempts have given the Christian faith an image to the unbelieving world of strenuous saintliness by men who were unconscious of what Jonathan Edwards termed "the labyrinthian depth of self-deception in the human heart." For the fact is that the self *can* be beguiled from its self-concern by being engaged in its affections, responsibilities, and creative concerns. But one cannot "deny" or "forget" the self by conscious and fretful preoccupation with the power of self-concern.

"The self is like an onion" is the well-known cry of the mystic, "you must peel off skin after skin of the onion and the self to eliminate it." But this is forgetting that the self is like the onion in another way than intended. For the onion is a vegetable which becomes more and more pungent as you peel off its innumerable layers and skins. The tears in the eyes of a cook who is peeling an onion are symbolic of the tears of pity and derision with which observers behold the sweaty and self-conscious efforts of conscious unselfishness. Furthermore, the pretensions of righteousness of these too conscious saints are an offense to the whole enterprise of morals in human history. For virtue which is not conscious of the mixture of motives in the human heart is bound to be as unimpressive to the observer as it is impressive to the deluded agent.

Two chapters of Christian history were informed by the passion of conscious selflessness. The oldest one, that of medieval asceticism, was rather impressive. But it is significant that medieval monasticism was most creative when, unfaithful to its principles of calculated selflessness, it dared the corruptions of the world in order to serve the culture of Europe with the monks acting as architects, teachers, manuscript copiers, and expert agronomists; in other words, as creators rather than as saints.

Although some may question the enterprise of calculated selflessness, it must be remembered that this rigorous effort at ascetic purity produced Francis of Assisi, whose lyrical quality of life refutes all strictures against monastic pretensions. Perhaps even St. Francis was deficient in the self-knowledge, which, rather than self-repression, is the first virtue of the truly religious life. There is the story of Francis fasting in repentance because the monks had violated one of the extremely rigorous rules of his order. Brother Elias, who was the Sancho Panza to Francis's Don Quixote, made the perceptive remark, "Brother Francis, are you so sorry because the brothers defied the will of God, or because they defied *your* will?" Thus, Brother Elias revealed that he was more aware than Brother Francis of the fact that even saints, and perhaps saints in particular, were inclined to identify their will with the ultimate norm of human existence. If this be true, the primary problem of human existence is the prevention of human idealism from becoming a screen and veil for all these "baser" impulses which the self refuses to acknowledge.

A less impressive venture in conscious selflessness was made by nineteenth-century liberal Protestantism. It was less impressive because it was not as rigorous as the medieval monks in dealing with the problem of alter-egoism, which the fact of family loyalty poses to the sensitive conscience. The Protestant saints, unlike the medieval saints, were not celibates for the sake of the kingdom of Heaven. Their ethical rigorism was partly drawn from the radical Reformation, which unlike the classical Reformation, criticized Catholicism, not for being too perfectionist, but for not being rigorous enough. Liberal Protestantism usually drew both from the radical Christian tradition, which placed emphasis on the promise, "If any man be in Christ, he is a new creature," and from the tradition of the rational enlightenment, which assumed that ignorant men were self-regarding but intelligent men were not, since the "reason" of man was the guarantor of the universal character of this sense of obligation to his fellowmen.

This curious combination of virtue guaranteed both by piety and by reason spread an aura of sentimentality and pretension over the political life of the nineteenth century, and obscured the obvious fact that the collective life of man, in the competition of races, classes, and nations, was a contest of power in which justice could only be achieved by an equilibrium of power. Only slowly did a liberal culture awake to the truth which it should always have known, a fact expressed by David Hume, namely that, while it was wise to make distinctions between selfish and unselfish men, the political realm would have to assume their collective self-regard.

The futility of the calculated quest for rigorous virtue brings us to the other, perhaps valid theme drawn by Christian faith from the drama of Christ's death on the cross. This theme rests on the improbable but profound assertion that the divine mercy, shining in and through the divine judgment, and which is revealed in this drama, can be appropriated only by those who cease to pretend to a purer virtue than is possible for man to possess, and instead acknowledge the devious ways of the human heart. Only those who know and understand the endless mixtures of love and self-love in all human creativity, are able to approach their fellowmen with compassion and forgiveness. This is the theme which the Reformation set against all the moral pretensions of medieval Christianity when it asserted that "God's grace is nothing but his forgiveness to sinners," and confessed with Luther that the final sin of man is his effort to prove himself sinless. It is the theme elaborated by Christ himself in his parable of the Pharisee and Publican which ends with the observation that "everyone who exalts himself will be humbled; and whoever humbles himself will be exalted," or in the parable of the unmerciful servant in which the lesson is driven home that only men who know themselves to be impure and forgiven in their impurity can treat their fellows with compassion.

The rigor with which the Reformation emphasized this gospel theme did not prevent many new forms of moral pretension from arising on the ground of the Protestant version of the Christian faith. Thus the history of Protestantism shows that a rigorous form of moral idealism is more popular than a rigorous form of self-knowledge. For the one may enhance the prestige of the good man, while the other threatens the cherished distinction between the good and evil men, proving us all to be brothers under the skin.

Yet distinctions between good and evil, between justice and injustice, between the honest teacher and the propagandist, between the responsible statesman and the irresponsible demagogue are very important, and must be made. Our precarious virtues and moral standards depend upon these careful judgments and distinctions. But the multifarious dramas of history reveal the provisional nature of these distinctions. Ultimately considered, evil is done, not so much by evil men, but by good men who do not know themselves.

One thinks immediately of the long history of fierce idealists from the "incorruptible" Robespierre and the Jacobins to Lenin and the Communists, who derived a cruel fanaticism from their fierce idealism. Even Cromwell, who in his evangelical moods was very conscious of the ambiguity of human virtue and admonished the Presbyterian divines, "in the bowels of Christ, think it possible you may be mistaken," could invade Ireland and wage cruel warfare in the name of an evangelical faith.

One of the most significant reinterpretations by Jesus of all the traditional eschatological symbols of the sharp distinction between justice and injustice, virtue and vice, was his reinterpretation of the apocalyptic story of the "last judgment," with the separation of the "sheep and the goats." According to Jesus, the righteous, who stood "on the right hand" of the Messianic judge, protested that they were not really virtuous—"Lord, when was it that we saw you hungry and fed you?"—while the unrighteous were equally unconscious of their deeds of omission and commission. This version of the last judgment prompted Pascal to the observation, "The world is divided between saints who know themselves to be sinners, and sinners who imagine themselves to be saints."

The ultimate mystery of good and evil negates our provisional distinctions, and must be accepted in contrite self-awareness before men can treat their fellowmen with any degree of compassion. It is so difficult to acknowledge and to accept for oneself that the Christian faith often has been distorted to present the climax of the Christian frame of meaning, the cross of Christ, as something less demanding than an invitation to honest self-analysis. In the patristic ages, Christian philosophers tried to show that "God was in Christ reconciling the world to himself" by proving that Jesus was really divine, was in historical fact the second person of the triune God. Theologians of all traditions and of all the ages have tried to reduce the grand drama of Christ's death on the cross to an objective historical fact in which you must believe in order to be saved. You are "saved," they have asserted, only if you believe that you "are washed in the blood of the lamb."

Surely Martin Buber is right in the thesis of his "two types of faith," when he declares that this second type of faith translates faith into "belief in" and makes belief in historically improbable propositions into a guarantee of "redemption in an unredeemed world." Naturally, there are many evasions and corruptions—theological, metaphysical, and historical—of the main burden of the Christian gospel, because that main theme is an affront to the pride of virtuous men, and an invitation to a kind of religious experience which is more painful than all philosophical speculation and moral pretension.

But an acceptance of this main theme of the drama of the cross naturally raises the question as to whether it negates or subordinates the other theme of rigorous striving for moral perfection. The answer is that it does not. It makes the ultimate moral attitude toward our fellows more possible and freer of pretension. All of Jesus' teachings on forgiveness declare in effect that only God and sinful men, that is, men who are aware of their sins, can be forgiving to their fellowmen. That is the point of the parable of the unmerciful servant.

The final mystery of good and evil in life and history is in fact that love, compassion toward our fellowmen, which is the ultimate good according to our Christian faith, cannot be achieved by strenuous striving; rather, it is achieved by an honest self-scrutiny and self-awareness which discovers affinities between the foe's obvious weaknesses and our hidden vices. Surely this is a truth which is applicable to our collective, as well as to our individual, life, though nations are notoriously self-righteous and lacking in organs of self-analysis. An obvious example is the division of the world into good and evil classes and nations, and the equally absurd notion which makes the "good" Communists the inheritors of the final victory of history. But it is equally obvious that our weaknesses have been drawn from the same source of moral pretension, of being the leaders of the so-called "free world," of regarding Western democracy, elaborated in the favorable circumstances of European history, not as a luxury which other cultures may or may not afford, but as the final norm of human existence.

Surely there is an ironic quality in the contest between the superpowers of our day, each of whom are inclined to hide their natural power impulses behind the veil of messianic commitments. We only hope that this irony may give way to saving grace, so that the powerful nations may find a bridge across ideological gulfs. That bridge should be their common consciousness of the proleptic guilt of a nuclear catastrophe, together with their common responsibility for avoiding the catastrophe.

It may be too optimistic to expect the awful chasm of a nuclear age to be bridged by the ultimate in religious and moral experience. But even if it should not be, it still remains true that there is no way of observing and participating in the grand and awful drama of life without despair unless we can analyze ourselves without deception or illusion.

O God, in whose sight no man living is justified, pity our vanities and deceptions, our consequent cruelties and false judgments. Grant us the grace of honest self-knowledge, that we may not think of ourselves more highly than we ought to think. Knowing our frailty, we may, in compassion, join our fellows in the awesome pilgrimage of life.

12.   For Nation and Community

O God, who has ordained that all men should live and work together as brethren, remove, we humbly beseech you, from those who are now at variance, all spirit of strife and all occasion for bitterness that, seeking only what is just and equal, they may ever continue in brotherly union and concord. Lead us out of the night of this conflict into the day of justice. Give us grace to be instruments of the kingdom of love and justice in the affairs of mankind; and patience in dealing with all the sins and selfishness of men, and humility in recognizing our own, that we may judge wisely between a man and his brother, between nations and peoples, and, by composing their differences, build them up into a true community of nations.

Our Father, we thank you for all the provisions made for the needs of men, for the ordered course of nature and for the miracle of the abundance by which our life is sustained. Grant us grace to distribute this abundance, not according to the caprice of what nature has given to one and withheld from another, but according to your love for all your children. Most especially do we pray for your spirit upon this nation, that it may not perish in surfeit while much of the world perishes in need. Grant that we may have ears to hear and eyes to see the need of the anxious and troubled peoples of the world.

O Lord, unless you build the house, its builders will have toiled in vain. Unless you watch over the city, in vain the watchman stands on guard.

Look with mercy upon this company of your children that our labors may be crowned by your grace. Help us to be diligent in the disciplines of our calling and to engage in them in the fear of the Lord which is the beginning of wisdom. Bind us together through our common responsibilities and prevent by your grace the frictions of sinful purpose from destroying the unity of the body of Christ. Give us the spirit of forbearance with one another, teaching us to forgive one another, even as you also in Christ have forgiven us. Help us to do the duty which each hour and day demands of us, but grant us grace also to have a vision of the constancy of your will above the chances and changes of our mortal life. Let us not be tempted by our weakness to evade the tasks you have given us to do; nor be tempted by our strength to estimate ourselves too highly. Grant that your strength may be made perfect in our weakness and your mercy purify what we have corrupted. O Lord, rule and overrule our affections and wills, that your kingdom may come, even through the confusion of human passions, and your will be done despite the unruly affections of men.

Look with mercy upon the peoples of the world, so full both of pride and confusion, so sure of their righteousness and so deeply involved in unrighteousness, so confident of their power and so imprisoned by their fears of each other. Have mercy upon our own nation, called to such high responsibilities in the affairs of mankind. Purge us of the vainglory which confuses our counsels, and give our leaders and our people the wisdom of humility and charity. Help us to recognize our own affinity with whatever truculence or malice confronting us that we may not add to the world's woe by the fury of our own resentments. Give your Church the grace in this time to be as a saving remnant among the nations, reminding all peoples of the divine majesty under whose judgment they stand, and of the divine mercy of which they and we have a common need.

We pray for all who have authority in the world, for the leaders of our nation and for those who bear office in all the nations, that they may seek the peaceable fruits of justice; grant that they may know the limits of human wisdom in the perplexities of this day, and calling upon you in humility, and acknowledging your majesty, may learn the wisdom of restraint and the justice of charity.

Almighty God, our heavenly Father, guide, we beseech you the nations of the world into the ways of justice and truth and establish among them the peace which is the fruit of righteousness. Temper the pride of victors by the knowledge that your judgment is meant for victors and vanquished. Transfigure the despair of the vanquished into hope, and let not the pride of the victors obscure the mercy of the judge before whom they will be judged. Bind us together, victors and vanquished, uneasy partners and former enemies, into a new community and thus make the wrath of man to praise you.

O God, our refuge and our strength and very present help in trouble, we ask you to guide and protect our nation in the trials of variance and division. Grant us the grace of true repentance and take away the offenses of our people that we may become purer instruments of your will in history. Endow our leaders with courage and wisdom. Save us from cruelty, hatred, and malice. Remind us how dearly our securities are bought, whether in peace or war, at the price of other men's toil and blood. Make a speedy end of the tyrannies of the earth and cast down the mighty from their seats, exalting them of low degree. Deliver the desolate and oppressed of all the nations. Give patience and courage to all who suffer from the pride of race and nation. Whenever men are despised, grant them the sense of dignity which comes from knowing that they are your children. Hasten the advent of peace and understanding between all men, separated now by class, race, or nation. Grant us grace to achieve justice with our fellowmen by the exercise of every gift of the power of your providence, which can make the wrath of man to praise you.

We pray most particularly for those nations and peoples whose national life has been destroyed, whose cities lie in ashes and rubble, and whose spirits are tempted to despair. Give them and us grace to discern your will and judgments beyond the confusions and arrogance of our judgment upon them. Grant that the might of the victor will be tempered by mercy, so that bitterness and confusion be not increased. Give us grace to know that the power of the Lord is greater than our power, and above the divine power is the divine mercy.

We pray to you this day mindful of the sorry confusion of our world. Look with mercy upon this generation of your children so steeped in misery of their own contriving, so far strayed from your ways and so blinded by passions. We pray for the victims of tyranny, that they may resist oppression with courage and may preserve their integrity by a hope which defies the terror of the moment. We pray for wicked and cruel men, whose arrogance reveals to us what the sin of our own hearts is like when it has conceived and brought forth its final fruit. O God, who resists the proud and gives grace to the humble, bring down the mighty from their seats.

We pray for ourselves who live in peace and quietness, that we may not regard our good fortune as proof of our virtue, or rest content to have our ease at the price of other men's sorrow and tribulation.

We pray for all who have some vision of your will, despite the confusions and betrayals of human sin, that they may humbly and resolutely plan for and fashion the foundations of a just peace between men, even while they seek to preserve what is fair and just among us against the threat of malignant power. Grant us grace to see what we can do, but also to know what are the limits of our powers, so that courage may feed on trust in you, who are able to rule and overrule the angry passions of men and to make the wrath of men to praise you.

∽⌒∽

O Lord, our judge and our redeemer, grant that nations and peoples, wise men and fools, the righteous and the unrighteous may, above and beyond every judgment and redemption of history, discern the love which judges them and redeems them. O God, who has wounded us in our self-esteem, restore us to our true selves; O Lord of history, who has destroyed nations and empires in their pride, rebuild us at this time into a true community. Be with those peoples and nations who are seeking freedom and security in the aftermath of war.

∽⌒∽

O God, the sovereign of nations and the judge of men, look with compassion upon this sad world so full of misery and sorrow. Enlighten our eyes that we may see the justice of your judgments. Increase our faith that we may discern the greatness of your mercy. Save us from the sorrow of the world which works death and despair. Fill us with the godly sorrow which works repentance, and the desire to do your will. Teach us how we may build a common life in which the nations of the world may find peace and justice. Show us what we ought to do. Show us also what are the limits of our powers and what we cannot do. So may our purpose to do your will be supported by our faith, for you are able to overrule our will and to make the wrath of man to praise you. Recall us to our dignity as co-workers together with you. Remind us of our weakness that we may look to you who works in us both to will and to do your good pleasure and supplies what is needed beyond our powers.

Hear us as we pray to you in these tragic days of our history amid the tumults and alarms of war, when rulers fail and nations fall and you have cast the mighty from their seats, when you have made the judges of the earth as vanity and the nations appear as but a little thing before you. Grant us grace to hear the voice of your judgments in the sorrows and pains of our day, so that we may be awakened from sloth and heedlessness. Help us also to discern your grace within and above your judgment, that we may not be driven to despair. Thus, knowing both your justice and your mercy, we may not be as those who have no hope. Turn our sorrow into repentance and our repentance into firm resolution to do your will and to seek to build a fairer world.

We pray for all the suffering children of men:

For those who brave great peril in our behalf, make us mindful of our debt to them;

For the wounded and the dying, give them a vision of the meaning of life which transcends life and death;

For the victims of cruel tyranny that they may know how to assert the integrity of the spirit against malignant power.

Remind us of our dignity as children of God that we may not be tempted to cowardice;

Remind us of our weakness so that we may not corrupt the cause we defend by arrogance.

O Lord, who are able to make the wrath of man to praise you, rule and overrule the angry passions and sinful affections of men that we may be led out of this night of sorrow into a brighter day.

O Lord, guard those who guard us. Give them stout hearts and keep them from all cruelty or malice that no dishonor stain their power. Remind us how dearly our securities are bought, whether in peace or war, at the price of other men's toil and tears. Remind us all of your majesty which rules and overrules the ambitions and powers of men, that we and all your children be not discouraged in defeat nor arrogant in the day of triumph.

Lead the nations and all who have dominion in them to a new day in which your power which stands over the power of nations will be freely acknowledged, and men may find peace and justice through a concord of wills under your will which is justice and mercy for all men.

If you, O Lord, should mark iniquity, O Lord, who could stand? Enter not into judgment with your servants, for in your sight is no man living justified. Have pity upon us, O Lord, for all open and secret defiance of your will.

Cleanse us of our secret faults. Most especially we confess all temptations to arrogance and vainglory in the moment of triumph or in the hour of victory. Help all men to remember that the only sacrifice acceptable to you is a broken spirit and a contrite heart. Grant us, O Lord, the grace of true repentance. Help us to discern your judgments in the history of these years, and to know that judgment is measured both to victors and to vanquished alike. Give us grace to renew our life as men and as nations, so that we may not perish under the severity of your chastisements, but arise to newness of life and a larger charity by the persuasions of your mercy.

We thank you, our Father, for all the provisions made for the needs of the bodies and souls of men, for the ordered course of nature and for the miracle of the harvest by which our life is sustained. Teach us to distribute to all according to their need what you have intended for their sustenance. We thank you for our physical life, with its strength and gladness, and for the glimpses of the eternal which shine through human joys and woes. We praise you for the human mind and its power to survey the world in its length and breadth, and for the infinities of thought and truth which carry our imagination beyond our comprehension. We thank you, too, that the world which exceeds our comprehension is not lost in mystery, but that through seers and saints, and finally Jesus Christ, we have been given light upon the meaning of the mystery which surrounds you. Grant us grace to walk in humility and gratitude before you.

O Lord, forgive our sins. We confess our manifold iniquities to you; our greed and sloth, our luxury and wastefulness of your gifts, our disobedience of your laws, our indifference to the needs of others, the deafness of our ears to the cries of the hungry, the hardness of our hearts to the anguish of tormented men, our ruthlessness in competition, our enslaving of our fellowmen to mammon, our spoiling of our brother's soul. O Lord, cleanse our hearts and renew a right spirit within us so that our life and deeds may reflect your glory, and our sinful lives may become the vehicles of your grace.

Have mercy upon us, O Lord, for we defy your will all the day long. You have made us to serve each other and to become our true selves only as our lives are lost in the love of others. Yet we forget others and seek our own. Forgive the pride and arrogance in which we think more highly of ourselves than we ought to think. Forgive the needlessness by which we seek to establish our own life at the expense of others.

✿

In your presence, our Father, our hearts are moved to awe and gratitude, but also touched by a deep disquiet. All things are open before you, and no secrets are hid from your eyes. As we feel your eye upon us our own eyes are clarified, and we behold what we truly are.

Forgive us for being so deeply involved in deceit and in the secret betrayal of your love. The will indeed is present with us, but how to perform that which is good we know not. Break, O Lord, the chains of our self-love. Annul by your mercy all the hurt we have done others by our pride, envy, and deceit. In your power and wisdom redeem this generation of your children and bring us out of the tumult and misery of this day into a new and wider concord. But, above all, give us that peace which passes understanding, which the world cannot give or take away.

✿

O Lord, whose kingdom is not of this world but yet whose truth is the judgment seat before which we must all be made manifest, reveal yourself to us above and beyond the confusion of counsel in which we stand. Reveal yourself as our judge so that we may not be at ease if the world thinks well of us, nor be dismayed if it judges us severely. Your judgments are more severe and your mercy is greater than the justice and the goodness of the world. Grant us grace to submit ourselves to your will, that dying to our own desires, we may arise to newness of life.

13. The Burden of Conscience

Bear one another's burdens, and so fulfil the law of Christ. For if any one thinks he is something, when he is nothing, he deceives himself. But let each one test his own work, and then his reason to boast will be in himself alone and not in his neighbor. For each man will have to bear his own load.

Let him who is taught the word share all good things with him who teaches.

Do not be deceived; God is not mocked, for whatever a man sows, that he will also reap. For he who sows to his own flesh will from the flesh reap corruption; but he who sows to the Spirit will from the Spirit reap eternal life. And let us not grow weary in well-doing, for in due season we shall reap, if we do not lose heart. So then, as we have opportunity, let us do good to all men, and especially to those who are of the household of faith.

Galatians 6:2–10, RSV

From the Scripture lesson of the morning, the sixth chapter of the Epistle to the Galatians, I select two texts, seemingly contradictory. One is, "Bear one another's burdens, and so fulfil the law of Christ"; and the other is, "For each man will have to bear his own load."

Now these contrasting admonitions of St. Paul to the community in Galatia are contradictory not by inadvertence, nor by Paul's incapacity for logical thinking. They happen to be relevant to two

Union Theological Seminary, New York, April 23, 1967.

dimensions of human existence. I am going to use spatial and mathematical symbols for these two dimensions. First, there is the horizontal symbol which indicates the social substance of human existence and the social character of human existence: "Bear one another's burdens."

We are all mixed up with our society. We are indebted to all communities, beginning with the family, for what we hold dear. We are dependent upon all communities, beginning with the family and ending with the community of mankind, for what we aspire to, and we are responsible to all communities for our actions. This is the social and universal substance of mankind. It is what makes us all brothers.

The other dimension is vertical. The symbol of vertical dimension is suggested by the words of St. Paul, "Let each one test his own work." He is saying, Do not think any more highly of yourself than you ought to think. Do not think that you are something when you are nothing. And then finally, "Do not be deceived; God is not mocked, for whatever a man sows, that he will also reap." This is the idea of an ultimate judgment.

The vertical dimension, with its ultimate apex of faith, expresses our individual existence. We are gloriously both universal and unique. Nobody else is quite like us. The police can discover us by our fingerprints—not that the fingerprints are the cause of our unique personality—but they are certainly a symbol. The vertical dimension is in a way the most obvious religious dimension, and we can explain it better by the symbol of transcendence than by the statement of rational philosophy, according to which man is distinguished from animals because he is a rational creature.

Reason is the instrument of our transcendence. Man lives in nature, yet transcends nature, and builds history in his communities, and then he transcends these communities of history and has his own conscience, whereby he can judge the historical situation. Finally, looking higher to a more transcendent level, he feels himself subject to an ultimate judgment. This is man under the judgment of God, making what Kierkegaard calls the "leap of faith." The German existentialist philosopher, Karl Jaspers, more correctly calls it the assumption that there is a source and end of meaning which transcends all our particular meanings. The great Jewish philosopher, Martin Buber, echoes this view when he says all prophetic faith rests upon the assumption that the God whom I meet in my conscience is the creator of the whole world.

These, then, are the two dimensions. I would like to trace the dimension of mutual responsibility first in the horizontal dimension and then in the vertical dimension, where it is conscience—the uneasy conscience, or a sense of sin. A sense of sin means that we transcend our own actions, so that we can say to ourself, "I haven't really done as well as I ought to." Our reach is always beyond our grasp.

When we consider the first dimension, the social character of human existence, we realize that we owe everything to everybody, beginning with the family, that we are indebted to them, that we are fulfilled in them, and that we are responsible for them. We cannot really elaborate this thesis of mutual responsibility without making a distinction between the two forms of universality that we as human beings possess. We are universal as creatures who have need of food and shelter, perhaps locomotion and communications in modern existence, and we are dependent upon each other for these goods. Secondly, we are free spirits with a certain dignity and we must carry each other's burdens; the strong, particularly, must carry the burdens of the weak in order to guard the dignity of our humanity. This is the point of "Bear one another's burdens."

There is, however, a note of perfectionism in St. Paul's admonition, "Bear one another's burdens, and so fulfil the law of Christ." For St. Paul the law of Christ was perfect mutual love and perfect sacrificial love, simultaneously and alternatively. Is that possible for the individual? Is it possible for communities? There are very few communities which fulfill the law of Christ.

St. Paul, however, was also a realist, and he often expressed the minimal condition of righteousness, or the minimal condition of man's ability to live at peace with his fellows. "If possible, as far as it depends upon you, live peaceably with all." This is a more modest goal than thinking we can really fulfill the law of Christ.

St. Paul as a realist was a father of the Reformation; and as a perfectionist he was the father of all perfectionist sects. But perfectionism is too simple for the problem of carrying each other's loads in the history of human economy, from primitive barbarism to our advanced technical civilizations. If we look at our economic history, we might say we have done everything we could to harness the self-will and self-interest of man. That is the basis of our American free-enterprise system. We harness self-interest for the sake of the whole. We deflect self-interest but encourage competitive strivings; and then we make great moral and legal decisions of discriminative justice between the competitive claims.

This is a rather wonderful history of man, wonderful and terrible. We might say, "Isn't it terrible that we are so persistently selfish, particularly collectively? And isn't it grand that we always have some sense of community—the nation, the family, the church, the community of mankind—in which we incorporate all of these self-regarding impulses?" Such is the terror and the glory of human history.

On the second level of bearing each other's burdens, the horizontal level, there is the example of the civil rights movement. A century after our Civil War—one wonders how we slept that long—through the Supreme Court decisions and the Negro revolution, we have finally decided that the white majority will carry the burdens of the black minority, which has been robbed of its dignity and respect as human beings. All kinds of strategems have been used. We do not persuade people that they must love each other. But, by law, we ordain that white children and black children shall study together and perhaps they will learn to understand each other. The law tries to master collectively embodied evil, as opposed to the evil in our own hearts.

When the American air force was integrated during the Second World War, a London paper published a dialogue with a Negro sergeant. The sergeant said, "Down home they say that the law can never change people's hearts, but the air force does a darned good job in making life tolerable for me." Blessed be the majesty of the law!

The issue of civil rights also gave us good illustrations of the vertical dimension of conscience. Two years ago when white racists threw a bomb into a Negro church and wrecked it and murdered three little Negro girls, a young lawyer named Charles Morgan wrote to the Birmingham paper. He said, "We are all guilty of this murder. Our racial pride has begotten us this racial hatred, and the racial hatred finally, when it was full-blown, became murder."

We know what happened after his expression of conscience. He lost his law practice, and he had to move because his family was threatened. A member of this seminary community who was a friend of Mr. Morgan's asked him, "How did it feel to be a traitor to the white race in one moment and a hero in the whole community the next moment?" And Mr. Morgan said, "You know, I never thought about that. I was so distressed by the threats to my children that I said to myself, 'If you had measured the ultimate consequences of the action, would you have written that letter?' " The conscience of the individual has its security and its insecurity in this terrible and wonderful world.

In the vertical dimension there is not only a sense of conscience but a sense of guilt. For we stand under an ultimate judgment that judges even our best work. John Donne knew that all of our intricacies of wrongdoing are ultimately connected with our fear of death, which is not the fear of dying, but the fear of meaninglessness.

> Wilt thou forgive that sin where I begun,
>   Which was my sin, though it were done before?
> Wilt thou forgive that sin, through which I run,

And do run still: though still I do deplore?
When thou hast done, thou has not done,
For, I have more.

Wilt thou forgive that sin which I have won
Others to sin? and, made my sin their door?
Wilt thou forgive that sin which I did shun
A year, or two: but wallowed in, a score?
When thou hast done, thou hast not done,
For I have more.

I have a sin of fear, that when I have spun
My last thread, I shall perish on the shore;
But swear by thyself, that at my death thy son
Shall shine as he shines now, and heretofore;
And, having done that, Thou hast done,
I fear no more.

If we analyze the different dimensions of human existence, the social and the vertical, we come to the disquieting conclusion that the roots of religious imagination are much more in the intensities of consciousness and conscience and sense of guilt than they are in all our social experience. Most of our social experiences, practically speaking, tend to idolatry, whether the idolatry of nation or denomination. As we pray together, we pray together idolatrously asking God to bless *us:* "Me and my wife, John and his wife, us four, no more."

Therefore I want to suggest that social sensitivity can be derived from the conscience of our individual religious life. Without some sensitivity we would not go through all the mechanics of justice required to bear one another's burdens; the nicely calculated less and more, the mechanics of an equilibrium of power between the trade union and the management, and the arbitration of strikes. But I would suggest that however self-contained might be our religion, and this is particularly true of Protestant individualism, there must be some frame of meaning in which even the individual Christian can look at the community, at our nation, for instance, and say to it, "Beware of the illusion of omnipotence, for your great wealth and your great power betray you into stupidities." There should be something in our religious life itself, whether it is derived from social experience or from our conscience, that could say that to the nation.

Then there is the precious and precarious peace based upon the nuclear dilemma. How could we ever escape its lesson? Here we are at the climax of all human history, hoping it will not be the end. The balance of terror, as Winston Churchill has said, holds the twin brothers of survival and annihilation. Certainly the grand and awful drama which envelops all of us is more impressive for the religious imagination than is your and my little individual drama. What an ironic drama it is, of man who is a monster in his power, and is a worm in his lack of the power to save himself. Perhaps we must not distinguish too much between the vertical and horizontal dimensions of our life. We are all both free spirits and social creatures. So we must bear one another's burdens, and we must all bear our own burdens of conscience, of guilt, and of aspiration.

Give us grace, our Father, to measure the height of our dignity as free spirits, and the depth of our misery and the breadth of our responsibility. Judge us in our vanities and pretensions. Have pity on us, for only your infinite pity is adequate to the infinite pathos of human existence.

14. For the Community of Faith

O come, let us worship and bow down, let us kneel before the Lord our maker, for he is our God and we are the people of his pasture and the sheep of his hand.

Let us pray:

O God, who are infinite, eternal and unchangeable, glorious in holiness, full of love and compassion, abundant in grace and truth, all your works praise you in all places of your dominion. Your glory is revealed in the life of Jesus Christ our Lord. Therefore, we praise Father, Son, and Holy Spirit, one God blessed forever.

O Lord, look with mercy upon this congregation of your people, drawn together from every part of the earth, united in the worship of our Lord, divided by diversities of gifts; differences of custom, usage, and tradition and loyalties of language and nation. Grant us grace fitly to be joined together, to be obedient to your will and to serve one another with our several gifts. Enrich our common life through our diversities, and help us to keep the unity of the spirit in the bond of peace. May we by your mercy listen to each other in humility, and learn from each other with patience and diligence, so that our love may grow in all knowledge and discernment. Give us a sense of gratitude to all who serve us, and who give us the comfort and leisure for study by their special labors, so that we may not forget to bestow the more abundant honor upon those members of our community whose work is less obvious or apparent. This we ask through him who was among us as one who served.

Eternal God, whom the heavens can contain, but who loves to dwell with those who are of contrite heart, grant us this day your grace, so that we may be rid of the pride and self-righteousness by which we seek to impress ourselves and our fellowmen. May we come before you with a humble and a contrite heart, acknowledging the weakness of our flesh and the sin of our spirit, being glad that before you all thoughts are open, all desires known, and from you no secrets are hid. Help us to worship with gladness, knowing that though your judgments are terrible, your mercy is also great toward all who confess their sins in true humility. Hear our prayers and satisfy the yearning of our hearts.

Look with mercy, our Father, upon this company of your people, united in worship and in the desire to know your will. Strengthen our faith so that, though we are perplexed, we may not be perplexed unto despair. Unite us in spirit with the company of your people everywhere, so that, by your grace, we may be a strong fortress of faith against unbelief, of courage against faintheartedness, of the knowledge of the true God against idolatry of all who worship race, ruler, and nation or any other majesty. O God, whose service is perfect freedom, may your children be freed from the bondage of the world because they submit themselves in bondage to you.

Grant us grace, O Lord, that the praise we give you as we begin the day may suffuse the thoughts and actions of this day. Be with us as we do our work and meet our friends and co-workers, and study the Scriptures, and search out the riches of your wisdom. We praise you in our search after wisdom, recognizing treasures of mystery and wisdom which lie behind and beyond all truth we seek or discover. We give you praise even in doing the humblest task, if by your grace we do it so that it is as a part of the whole plan of life you have for your children. Grant us, O Lord, the strength to do your will.

✍·✍

Almighty and eternal God, creator of the world, judge and redeemer of men, who gives us the treasures of darkness and the hidden
riches of secret places, grant that we may know that you are the Lord,
and that there is none else beside.

We worship you in awe, for before the mountains were brought
forth or ever the earth and the world were formed, even from everlasting to everlasting you are God; while we bring our years to an end
like a tale that is told.

We worship you with contrite hearts, for in the light of your holiness all our righteousness is as filthy rags. Enter not into judgment
with your servants, for in your sight is no man justified.

We worship you with gratitude, for you have both formed and
reformed, created and redeemed us. We are fearfully and wonderfully
made and that our soul knows well. We are even more fearfully and
wonderfully redeemed by your love which bears our sins, and by your
mercy which assuages your wrath against our sins, but does not cancel
your commands upon our conscience. Therefore we fear and tremble
before you, and yet may be glad and released in your sight.

We worship you as a company who have been called by various and
diverse promptings of your spirit to the ministry of your word. Grant
us grace to separate the precious from the vile, that we may speak
boldly and humbly to suffering and perplexed men. Make us diligent
to learn how rightly to divide the word of truth. Grant that our love
may grow more and more in all knowledge and discernment, and that
all our knowledge may be informed by our love for you and your will
for men.

Give your benediction to the work of this school in the new year,
so that all who labor and work here may walk worthy of the vocation

wherewith they are called, with all lowliness and meekness, with long-suffering, forbearing one another in love, endeavoring to keep the unity of the spirit in the bond of peace, till we all come into the unity of the faith and of the knowledge of the son of God, unto a perfect man, unto the measure of the stature of the fullness of Christ.

Our Father, we give thanks for all your servants who have lived and died by the grace of the gospel, of whom the world is not worthy, who, having obtained a good report, received not the promise, for you provided a better thing for us, that they without us should not be made perfect. Seeing we are compassed about with so great a cloud of witnesses, grant us grace to lay aside every weight and the sin which does so easily beset us, and let us run with resolution the race that is set before us, looking to Jesus who endured the cross, making light of its disgrace for the sake of the joy that lay ahead.

Look with mercy upon this company of your people. You have called us out of many lands and places to serve you in the ministry of your word. Teach us rightly to divide the word of truth. Grant that our love may grow in all knowledge and discernment. Help us each to walk worthily in the vocation wherewith we are called, forbearing one another in love and endeavoring to keep the unity of the spirit in the bond of peace. Teach us to look not each at his own things, but at the things of the other, so that we may impart and receive from one another whatever gift of the spirit you have given to each. O Lord, bind us together in the body of Christ that we may grow unto a perfect man, unto the measure of the stature of the fullness of Christ.

We pray, O Lord, for your Church, that it may be healed of its divisions by your grace; that it may reach your word with courage to a sinful world, and may mediate with true charity your love and mercy to all men. Strengthen every ministry of reconciliation therein with your spirit. Grant that it may be a true community of grace in which the pride of race or nation is humbled, where the strong and mighty are brought to judgment, and the meek and lowly are lifted up. Make it more faithful to its Lord, and more instant to meet the needs of men.

ᴄᴏ∽ᴏ

Almighty God, we bring our praise and worship before you. You formed the earth and created man upon it; your hands stretched out the heavens, and your word commanded all their hosts.

Give us grace to walk humbly and save us from pretension and every arrogant folly. You have made us, and not we ourselves. Help us to remember the limits of our power and our wisdom, but help us, too, to do our duty within the limits of our power and our wisdom.

Teach us each day to ask what you would have us do, and help us to perform our tasks with diligence and humility. Give us grace in this fellowship to be helpful to each other in our several responsibilities. Save us from seeking to impress our fellows, or from being afraid of their judgments when we are sure what you would have us do. Help us to seek your word of truth and not to be content with the letter of the law, since it is the spirit which gives life. Help us to learn from the prophets and sages of every age, the men of faith who out of weakness were made strong, the men of learning who have sought rightly to divide the word of truth. Give us above all the spirit of love, for if we have all knowledge and understand all mysteries, and have not love it profits us nothing. Grant us to bear each other's burdens, and so fulfill the law of love.

O Lord, save your people. Save the nations from their arrogance and folly, and grant them grace to walk peaceably with each other. Save the strong, the secure, the successful, and the wise, that they glory not in their might nor in their wisdom. Save the weak and the debased and all who are victims of heedless and cruel men, and reveal to them the final court and judgment where those of low degree are exalted and the disbalance of the world redressed. Save us, O Lord, from our sins and our anxieties, and grant us so sure a hold upon your grace that the peace which passeth understanding may keep our hearts, and we be enabled to walk serenely through the tumults and trials of these days, redeeming the time because the days are evil.

Almighty God, our Father, look with mercy upon this congregation of your children, that we may worship you in spirit and in truth. We lift our hearts in gladness to you as we think of all the good things of life which we have from you. We come before you in humility as we remember all things we have done and left undone in defiance of your will and become conscious of all that has been remiss in our thoughts, words, and deeds.

Sanctify our prayers, purging them of all lusts and desires which separate us from you, and filling them with all good impulses which unite us to you. Give us grace to live our life this day in your presence, and to perform our duties in accordance with your will.

Teach us each day what you would have us do, and help us to perform our tasks with diligence and humility. Give us grace in this fellowship to be helpful to each other in our several responsibilities. Save us from seeking to impress our fellows, or from being afraid of their judgments when we are sure of your commandment for us. Look with favor upon this company of your people, bound together in the common tasks and disciplines of your Church. Help us to search for your word of truth diligently and not to be content with the letter of your word, since it is the spirit which gives life. Help us to profit from the prophets and sages of every age, the men of faith who out of weakness were made strong, and the men of learning who have sought rightly to divide the word of truth. Give us above all the spirit of love, seeing that if we have all knowledge and understand all mysteries and have not love, it profits us nothing. Grant us to be members one of another in the body of which Christ our Lord is the head.

Eternal God, creator and redeemer of men, we thank you for this new day and for all your mercies which reveal the constancy of your love toward your children. Grant us grace to begin this day in your fear and with your favor; to perform our tasks as unto you; to live with all who share our work and our common life in the spirit of charity and goodwill. Banish all fears from our hearts that we may know that peace which the world cannot give or take away. Awaken us from the sloth and sleep of sin and grant us the power to obey your will with steadfast purpose and resolute hearts.

O Lord, who has called us to be ministers of your word and mediators of your grace to men, help us to separate the precious from the vile, that we may be worthy instruments of your will. Save us from corrupting any word of your judgment or of your mercy by vain imaginations of our own. Make us humble as we read, hear, sort, and appropriate the testimonies of seers and prophets of all ages. We give thanks that we are heirs of all the ages and that our faith is sustained by a vast company of the living and the dead who have known you and proclaimed your mercy. We thank you that we are sons as well as heirs; and that each one may in his own way find access to the throne of grace.

O Lord, have pity upon this generation of your children. Grant us to understand the terrible judgments in which our world is involved so that they may be seen not as meaningless misery prompting despair, but may be recognized as your judgments upon men. Assuage the passions of brutal men and overcome the cowardice of those who are of faint heart. Grant us power and grace to resist evil, knowing that even though we ourselves are sinful men you have called us to be instruments of your justice. Reveal your wrath to those who defy you, and the tenderness of your mercy to those who have been visited by your wrath.

Have mercy upon distressed persons; upon those who are imprisoned or afflicted in mind, body, or estate. Have compassion upon the dying and upon those who stand in the fear of death, that they may know, whether they live or die, they are with you.

✤

Service

Let us praise God for the beauty of his creation and the greatness of his mercy:

Yours, O Lord, is the kingdom and the power and the glory. We praise you for the creation of this world, for the wonder of all living things, for the order and harmony in which your creation moves, for seedtime and harvest, summer and winter, day and night.

We praise you for the peace and the majesty of nature, for all the strategems of life with which your dumb creatures are armed; and for the humility they teach us, as each fits into his appointed place in your creation. We bless you for everything which supports our life and for your providence which maintains and preserves the world in order.

We praise you for the creation after long years of man whom you made in your own image that you might reign within his heart; and for every ministry of your love by which he is recalled from his waywardness, and recreated and purified.

We praise you for the glory shining through the sad and yet majestic history of our race; for saints and seers, made perfect through suffering; for men of stout hearts who have defied malignant power; for all who have been tender toward the hurt and the maimed; for prophets who have discerned your judgments and your mercy in the events of man's history, and have proclaimed the mysteries of your will to their fellows; we thank you above all for Jesus Christ, who has set before us the meaning of your righteousness and your love.

We praise and bless your glorious name, O Lord.

Let us intercede for all who are in special need of God's grace:

We pray, our Father, for the rulers and leaders of the nations: Give them the spirit of humility when they confront problems too great for their wisdom, and the spirit of justice in all their counsels.

We pray for the peoples of the world: Let not the trials of this day be meaningless to them or drive them to despair, but rather encourage them to repentance and newness of life in a larger fellowship with all of the nations.

We pray for the wounded and the dying and those who stand in the fear of death, for the prisoners and captives and all who are the victims of proud and cruel men. We remember also, before your throne of grace, all who suffer for us and defend our securities at the risk of their lives.

Have mercy, O God, upon the ministers of your word, that they may rightly divide the word of truth, preaching your wrath to the defiant and the tenderness of your mercy to those who are cast down.

Have mercy upon all your children who are in special distress of body or soul and teach them how all things may work together for good to those who love you.

Let us confess our sins:

If you, Lord, would keep account of sins, who, O Lord, could hold up his head? Enter not into judgment with your servants, for in your sight no man living is justified.

We have worshiped ourselves and not given you the glory, we have changed the glory of God into the image of corruptible man, we have exalted our nation and race, our possessions and our comforts, our virtues and our achievements. Deliver us from all vanities which have dominion over us, and grant us grace to find freedom in your service, and newness of life in the death of the old self.

Eternal God, so rule our lives by your spirit, that all our thoughts, desires and ambitions, being made obedient to your will, your kingdom and your power and glory, may be made manifest in us and through us, through Christ our Lord.

Let us confess our sins:

Look with mercy upon us, our Father, for the multitude of our iniquities, for the pride with which our generation sought to build a new world, and for the despair with which we behold our world in ruins;

Lord, have mercy upon us.

For the complacency of all the nations who were not grieved when wounded by your judgment, and did not receive correction when consumed by your anger;

Lord, have mercy upon us.

For the self-righteous fury of victorious nations, and their inhumanity toward the vanquished;

Lord, have mercy upon us.

For the deafness of our ears to the cries of the needy, and for the vainglory to which our power tempts us;

Lord, have mercy upon us.

For the discord we create between nations and individuals by our desire of dominion over our fellowmen, and by our resentment of the hurts which our fellows inflict upon us, and our unconsciousness of the pains we have inflicted upon them;

Lord, have mercy upon us.

For the involvement of your church in the sins of the world, for its cowardice in tempering your judgments so that men be not grieved; for mixing the vainglorious opinions of men with the truth of your gospel, and for all lack of charity which has brought the prejudices of Jew and Gentile, and the chasm between bond and free, into the community of grace where all men should be one in Christ;

Lord, have mercy upon us.

For the despair which corrupts our faith in the day of calamity, as for the complacency which shrouded your word to men in the day of ease;

Lord, have mercy upon us.

O Lord, hear the prayers of our confession and grant that our sorrow may be a godly sorrow which leads to repentance and newness of life.

Service

"Without faith, it is impossible to please him; for anyone who comes to God must believe he exists and that he rewards those who search for him" (Hebrews 11:6).

Grant us, O Lord, the gift of faith, so that amid the confusions and perplexities of this life we may lay hold upon your power and your love. We search for you, but how can we find you unless you first have found us? We thank you for every revelation of yourself which pierces the chaos of human history, and for every light which shines in our darkness.

"By faith Abraham obeyed the call to go out to a land destined for himself and his heirs, and left home without knowing where he was to go" (Hebrews 11:8).

O God, the Lord of all ages, who has made us the creatures of time, so that every tomorrow is an unknown country, and every decision a venture of faith, grant us, frail children of the day, who are blind to the future to move toward it with a sure confidence in your love, from which neither life nor death can separate us.

"By faith Abraham settled as an alien in the land promised him, living in tents, . . . for he was looking forward to the city with firm foundations, whose architect and builder is God" (Hebrews 11:9).

You have given your children, as to Abraham, many lands of promise, periods of peace and just communities; grant that we trust not these immediate securities but that we may live therein in tents, as did Abraham; grant us grace to build our cities here on earth more soberly, because we know ourselves to be pilgrims and strangers here, desiring a better country.

"By faith Moses . . . refused to be called the son of Pharaoh's daughter, preferring to suffer hardship with the people of God rather than enjoy the transient pleasures of sin" (Hebrews 11:23).

O, Lord, who has set us amid constant temptations to choose the security and treasures of Egypt rather than the trials of the wilderness, help us to overcome all softness and every inclination to evade difficult choices. Teach us not to be too careful or prudent, but to remember him who had nowhere to lay his head.

"Time is too short for me to tell the stories of Gideon, Barak . . . of David and Samuel and the prophets. Through faith, they overthrew

kingdoms, established justice, . . . their weakness was turned to strength" (Hebrews 11:32).

Our Father, look with pity upon us too weak for the tasks which are set before us, unable fully to obey your commands or to discern your will. Grant us, by faith, a wisdom beyond our wisdom, that in your light, we may see light; and also a measure of your strength, which is made perfect in our weakness. So, amidst all that is fragmentary and contrary in our existence here, we may lay hold upon your grace, which completes what is incomplete, and corrects what is amiss.

"With all these witnesses to faith around us like a cloud, we must throw off every encumbrance, every sin to which we cling, and run with resolution the race for which we are entered" (Hebrews 12:1).

We praise you, our Father, for all these witnesses whose faith supports our faith and whose faithfulness gives us steadiness. We give praise for the holy company of martyrs and saints, of just men made perfect, for the fellowship of faith in its witness throughout the ages.

Prayers for Holy Communion

May we in this hour partake of the broken bread of truth and the poured wine of fellowship so that the horizons of our minds may be enlarged, our sympathies quickened, our imaginations fed and our spirits disciplined by new responsibilities and duties. Then may we come more fully into our heritage as children of God and as servants of the spirit.

May we have the grace of humility and contrition so that we may know ourselves for what we are and the courage to be loyal to what we ought to be, the discernment to make goodwill effective, and the goodwill to overcome self-will.

⚋⚋

We praise you for the life of the spirit, for the bread of life which you have given to those who hunger and thirst after righteousness, and for the living water which quenches the thirst of the soul. We thank you for the light of your truth and love which pierces through the darkness of our world and for your commandments which resolve our perplexities amidst conflicting duties. O Lord, give us grace both to give and to be satisfied with every portion of the bread of life.

⚋⚋

Service for Baptism

Dearly beloved, we are come together in the presence of God and of all the company of heaven to offer unto him our praise and thanksgiving for this miracle of birth; to pray for this child and for those to whom she has been given, that she and they may walk the way of your commandments and be made partakers of your heavenly kingdom.

"Hear, O Israel: The Lord our God is one Lord; and you shall love the Lord your God with all your heart, and with all your soul, and with all your might. And these words which I command you this day shall be upon your heart; and you shall teach them diligently to your children, and shall talk of them when you sit in your house, and when you walk by the way, and when you lie down, and when you rise." (Deuteronomy 6:4–7.)

"You shall love your neighbor as yourself. . . . The stranger who sojourns with you shall be to you as the native among you, and you shall love him as yourself; for you were strangers in the land of Egypt: I am the Lord your God." (Leviticus 19:18, 34.)

"On these two commandments hang all the law and the prophets" (Matthew 22:40).

"Suffer the little children to come unto me, and forbid them not: for of such is the kingdom of God" (Mark 10:14).

Thanksgiving.

Question to parents.

Baptism.

This child is now received into the family and fellowship of faith, in the good hope that she may grow in grace and show forth the riches of her heritage.

Let us pray:

Eternal God, the author of life, under your providence the miracle of birth is continually enacted. Yet when a new life is entrusted to us we behold the miracle with a new sense of awe and gratitude.

Merciful Father, who redeems us from evil and sin, even as you have created us, grant us grace to seek your redemption, even as we praise you for your creation.

Look with grace upon these parents who present this child for baptism that the vows which they make in its behalf may be spoken from hearts consecrated to your love and dedicated to their duties as parents. We give thanks that you have entrusted this life to them. Give them grace to guard it from evil but also to know that finally you alone can guard it. Endow them with a loving and devout spirit that in their home this child may grow into the full measure of the stature of Christ and also come to know the divine mercy by which all men are saved.

Prayers for a Marriage Service

Dearly beloved, we are met in the sight of God and in the presence of these witnesses to join this man and this woman in the holy estate of matrimony, which is an honorable estate, instituted for the comfort and continuance of mankind. It is therefore not to be entered into lightly but reverently, thoughtfully and in the fear of the Lord. Let us, therefore, invoke the blessings of God upon this union, begun this hour by their covenant.

Let us pray:

Eternal God, who has set the solitary in families and ordained that a man shall leave his father and his mother and cleave unto his wife, and they shall be one flesh; under your providence these your children have found, and learned to love and cherish each other. Grant your children grace, that the solemn vows said this day may surely be performed by everything that knits their lives together, by shared tasks and common interests, by sharing each other's joys and sorrows and by bearing common responsibilities and cares.

May their emotions of love, springing from their hearts, nourish the will to integrity, which is more constant than any emotion and is both the crown and servant of love.

O God, who has made us co-workers with you and introduced us to the awesome mystery of creation, bless this union with children; and grant their parents the wisdom, imagination, and patience to nurture new life in all goodness and godliness and every grace of life.

Our Father, who knows the weakness of our nature, give these your children the spirit of gratitude for each other's virtues and good intentions, and forbearance of each other's frailties and foibles, that the years may continue to strengthen their union, and time may add to its glory and its grace.

15. The Hazards and the Difficulties of the Christian Ministry

The difficulties which face the Christian minister are my subject. Without wanting to echo the words of Winston Churchill about blood, sweat, and tears, perhaps we can establish something like the tests of Gideon. He was told by the Lord in the day of crisis to proclaim to his people, "Whoever is fearful and trembling, let him return home." It may be that the stouthearted will be attracted to the ministry and the fainthearted be shooed away from it.

First, there is the fact of our calling. There must be a sense of vocation. A specific and isolated divine call to enter the ministry is not so important as a realistic understanding of what is involved in the Christian faith, and our personal commitment to it.

Biblical faith is based on, and presupposes, a sense of mystery beyond the world of intelligibility. The world has all kinds of structures, relationships, coherences, sequences, and systems which can be analyzed by the intellect, but beyond which there is mystery. Somehow or other, God dwells in this mystery. If anybody thinks that the world is self-sufficing, and self-explanatory, and self-fulfilling, he is very far from the Christian faith. But the Christian faith is not just a reaction to mystery. For in the Christian faith, that is, the biblical faith, it is presumed and affirmed that there is meaning in the mystery, and that the meaning is disclosed by a whole series of disclosures

Address for the Conference on the Ministry, Union Theological Seminary, New York, March 29, 1953.

which culminated in Christ. The Christian faith also declares that at the very foundation of the mystery is the creative action of God; that God is creator. But it is significant that while this comes first in the Bible, it is an afterthought with the prophets and with the New Testament. The prophets declared that this mysterious God called Israel out of Egypt. It is the same mysterious God who is disclosed in Christ. Then, as an afterthought, we say that this is the same mystery which was in creation.

So the mystery of creation is related to the mystery of God's disclosure in history. Mystery and disclosure do not exclude each other. The prophet Isaiah alternated in emphasizing the hiddenness of God, "My thoughts are not your thoughts," and the disclosure of God, "He has not spoken in a secret place but he has spoken ultimately." From the New Testament standpoint, God has spoken in many places that are incandescent points in history, where the mystery is revealed as meaning, in modern parlance, existentially. In a final way, he spoke by the sign that is, for the Christian, a supreme and climactic disclosure in Christ. Disclosure and mystery belong together; disclosure never completely dissolves mystery. One of the hazards of the Christian ministry is the pretension of knowing more about God than anybody has a right to know, to be a pretender into the privacy of God. I remember when I was a young parson, two Sunday school girls were playing under the window of my study. One said, "Let's not make too much noise; we will disturb Mr. Niebuhr." And the other little girl said, "Who is Mr. Niebuhr?" The first child answered, "Don't you know? He is the pastor in this church. He knows all about God." This shocked me, but reminded me of the pretenses to which the ministry is prone.

The same God who discloses himself as God the Father is the creator. God the Son is the supreme revealer. And this is the same mysterious God whom we encounter as Holy Spirit in all the times of our life when at the ultimate fringe of our consciousness, introspec-

tion and meditation are turned into a dialogue. Here is one of the
principal points of biblical doctrine: that in meditation we are not just
dipping into the depths of our unconscious until we have reached the
divine level, but that finally there is a dialogue, with another; the other
we call the Holy Spirit. The dialogue goes on constantly. I have to
comprehend and find Christ in the dialogue. The same God who is
Christ is the same God who is the Holy Spirit. I comprehend the
mystery not primarily by intellectual effort. I cannot think myself into
the Christian faith. I can indeed think myself out of it, but not into
it, because I have a mind with which I analyze the structures and
coherences of the world; but I am not primarily mind. You are not
primarily mind, but a self; and the encounter between yourself and
God involves not so much intellectual astuteness as repentance and
faith of the whole person.

Repentance is the basis for faith, because when I face the ultimate
situation in the dialogue with God, I find that I am making too much
of a claim for myself. This is the perpetual human situation. We are
all creatures who have this peculiarity. We are in the flux of events,
and yet we transcend them enough to know that we are in the flux,
and to be worried about it. So we pretend that we are not in it, that
we have a mind which transcends it, that we have a power or a virtue
which can defy death. The basic sin which is discovered in the encounter with God in Christ is the sin of pretension and pride. I think I am
a good man. I pretend that I am a virtuous man, and a wise man, until
I confront God in Christ, and then I know that I am in the wrong
before him because of all these pretenses. I have completed my life
falsely from the standpoint of myself, on the basis of my pride. So it
is necessary that I die to my own self if I would truly live. The
encounter with Christ always is an encounter which results in dying
to live. It is another aspect of the biblical faith: I have to die to myself,
but not in order that I might achieve some universal self, because I
am always going to be a particular self. It is a mystical or rationalistic

illusion that you can extricate some universal self from the particular self. Biblical faith is expressed in the words, "I am crucified with Christ. Nevertheless, I live." If we are crucified to the self which is centered around itself, if we are drawn out of ourself into love of neighbor and love of Christ, we truly live. Life is a perpetual Lent and Easter. It has to be perpetual because we are always falling into new forms of self-centeredness.

This paradox is not always understood. If I am in Christ, as St. Paul says, I am a new creature; I live no longer for myself but for God in Christ and for my fellowman. But if I look at myself very carefully, I know that I am not a new creature at all, because the old self is a very stubborn self; if I check it at one point, it expands to another point. That is why the Reformation insisted that the grace of God is not merely the power of Christ in us, but it is the mercy of God towards us, that is, forgiveness. Nothing is more insufferable than a professional holy man in a pulpit who pretends to all the Christian virtues. He is a pathetic sinner, this fellow; he may have entered the ministry because he is an exhibitionist at heart. One of the hazards about the ministry is that the more successful you are, the more you will be subject to various temptations of pride and exhibitionism. I can give myself in one moment to a cause of the word of our Lord, and then I can discover in the next moment that I have not given myself at all, but that the self stands outside in this process of self-giving, and asks, "Does anybody notice me in my virtues, or will they give proper credit for it?" Unless, on the one hand, we obey the biblical injunction to be like Christ, and on the other hand, know that we can never be like Christ, we have not mastered the difficulty of the Christian life.

There is much talk about pessimism and optimism in regard to human nature. The Christian faith has no illusions about human nature. But the only trick (and this applies particularly to the preacher of this gospel of dying to live) is that when you look at human beings and are disillusioned about their pretensions of virtue, you must look also at yourself and not have illusions about yourself. If you have illusions about yourself, you will be driven into cynicism by your disillusionment with your fellowman. We have to note, as Pascal said, that the misery of man is closely related to the dignity of man. We know it by analyzing ourselves rather than our fellowmen. If you look at yourself carefully, and particularly in the hour of prayer, you ought not to have any illusions about yourself, because you realize how persistent is this self-seeking, this pride and pretension of the self, even while you are preaching a sermon, or perhaps particularly then. Christian preaching is not so much teaching about what Christians ought to do, but it is the induction and the enrichment of people in the Christian faith through sermons, through pastoral experience, through private prayer, and the common prayers and worship of the church. All this must be done with the idea of confronting people with Christ, and being oneself confronted. To confront other people without being confronted oneself leads to insufferable pretensions of righteousness.

If this be near to a true analysis of the gospel upon which the Christian Church is founded, we have two difficulties: the practical difficulty of maintaining the uniqueness of the truth of this gospel against the claims of the world, and the intellectual problem to maintain it against the legitimate preoccupations of a scientific age.

The practical difficulty of preaching this gospel is that it seems least relevant to those people and to those generations to whom it is most relevant. From the standpoint of the gospel, we must regard power, or the wisdom or the security of any man as not being as significant as he tries to make himself believe that it is. The successful minister is in greater temptation, because he is more likely to deal with the powerful, the rich, the secure, and the wise. The gospel has a revolutionary transmutation of values: the maimed, and the halt, and the blind will enter the kingdom of God before all the "good" people, because they know life must be broken; while those who are secure with some form of philosophy, or power, or political sagacity, do not believe that life has to be broken. They do not think that the gospel is relevant. But it is just for them that it is relevant. Part of the task of preaching the gospel is to persuade those people, who think that the gospel is for the weak, that it is for the strong as well; that a strong man is really very weak. He cannot complete his own life, but God has to complete it. Nathan, the prophet, stood before David, the king, to challenge his sin with Bathsheba. David, in his pride, could not be convicted of sin; so the prophet told a parable of a wealthy man who took a ewe lamb away from a poor man. The king was aroused to a fury of self-righteousness as he condemned the sin of another man. "The man . . . shall surely die." The prophet spoke, sticking in the stiletto, "Thou art the man." This is how one must practice guile in preaching the gospel to people who will not believe it.

Preaching the gospel involves practical difficulties, particularly in a day like ours and in a nation such as ours, with all of its power and wealth. We are a virtuous nation, except from the ultimate standpoint. To persuade this virtuous nation that in the ultimate instance it is not virtuous is to run the danger of being called pro-Communist. We are a virtuous nation compared to a tyranny; and we may have to risk our life in order to save these virtues. But in the sight of God, our nation is in a very precarious position with all of its self-congratulation. Individuals are related to God and they know of his judgment and mercy, but nations as nations, do not. This should not make us Christian individualists who have no concern for our civilization or nations. But we have to face the fact when we preach the gospel in a great and powerful nation like ours, which combines the perils of a righteous nation with the perils of a powerful nation. These are some of the practical difficulties which we face in preaching the gospel to the secure, the rich, and the wise, whether among people or nations.

For these reasons, the ministry is a dangerous calling. You realize that people really secretly desire that the minister help them to ease

an uneasy conscience. They know that they are not as good or as
powerful as they pretend to be, and they would like to have somebody
tell them that they are. Who would be more plausible for this task of
deception than the preacher? It is very difficult to preach the gospel
honestly. It means to preach the severity of God to the proud, and
the mercy of God to the brokenhearted. To preach honestly and not
to cut the corners is not easy to do. After a sermon, how often was
I conscious of the fact that, on the one hand, I was trying to be, as
we said in those days, a "prophetic voice." On the other hand, as I
glanced over my congregation, I saw this fellow here and that fellow
there, and I began to speculate with myself: Could not I put what I
have to say just a little bit differently so that this fellow would not be
quite as offended as he will be if I put it bluntly? I might be tempted
to "temper the wind to the shorn sheep." If any minister thinks he
is free of that temptation, he is going to fall into it.

A preacher is the mediator of God's judgment and also of his
mercy. He may claim to preach with great courage; but he also must
recognize how he is himself involved in the sins against which he is
preaching. Mercy, humility, and charity must come out of this recognition. We must face the hazard of cowardice; also the pretensions of
courage without charity. The older I grow in the ministry, the more
I am impressed by good pastors who do not necessarily specialize in
the word of God from the pulpit. That is a hit-or-miss affair in any
event, because it has to deal with the severity and the goodness of
God, and you have to distinguish somewhat between those who must
be broken before they can be rebuilt, and those who are broken and
must be rebuilt; between judgment and mercy. That is the pastoral
task and only a man of great humility and charity can help all these
wandering and confused people. The scattering shot of the pulpit is
not nearly as valuable as the pastoral work with individual souls.

Now, let us consider the intellectual difficulties of preaching. Not
only from the standpoint of a scientific age or from the standpoint of
metaphysics is the gospel neither rational nor scientific. You cannot

teach the Bible without understanding its historical character. The prophets spoke to a particular historical situation. This is the "scandal of particularity," as theologians call it. We affirm that a timeless truth was spoken by the prophets or by Christ at a particular moment in time. St. Paul used the same word, the "scandal" or trap, when he expounded the gospel, the good news that God, the eternal God, the mysterious God, is revealed in this one particular event, the cross and the resurrection of Christ. The gospel is the foolishness of God against the wisdom of the world. As St. Paul said truly, the world by its wisdom does not know God. The world by its wisdom knows all the structures of reality, but it cannot penetrate to the ultimate mystery; it does not know God.

The Christian gospel is a gospel of history and revelation. It is the only way truth can be revealed as coming from an eternal selfhood to my selfhood. We are organisms and structures which have been analyzed scientifically; and we are also free spirits who rise indeterminately in our freedom, indeterminately over the structures of the world and of time and the flux of history, to meet God. We are images of God. He has a freedom that is at least as great as ours. This mysterious freedom of the self can be comprehended only in history. If you and I dealt with each other scientifically, we would correlate our behavior according to patterns. We would say, "This fellow is a middle-class person. He has this and that prejudice," et cetera, and we would put ourselves in categories, psychological and sociological. That is scientific analysis of our human selfhood. All of it is legitimate as far as it goes; but finally, you and I are persons. I cannot know you if you do not speak to me out of the depths of your personal unity and transcendence. I can make all kinds of guesses about your behavior, but probably they will be false. I make guesses about God's behavior in the world but they are false unless God speaks out of his freedom to my freedom. This is why history is of revelational importance in human life.

There are structures which the scientists analyze empirically and the philosophers, metaphysically. We must not deny that there are structures on every level, more obviously on the level of nature. But the metaphysical enterprise is justified also, for are there not some superstructures besides these structures that we analyze empirically? Much of our culture was established by the scientific and philosophical discipline that arose with the Greeks. In the world of the universities and generally in the world of culture, we are among the heirs of this tradition. The Bible may seem outdated or irrelevant. So it is difficult to maintain the incandescent points of evangelical Christianity against the distractions of metaphysical and scientific disciplines. If you are going to be a Christian thinker and leader, you will be caught in the debate as to how you can do justice to the biblical, that is, to the historical and personal side of the Christian faith, and also do justice to the obvious structures of the world, including the structures that some psychologists can analyze in your own psyche.

If you do not relate this faith to the structures of the world, as analyzed by science and metaphysics, the Christian faith may degenerate into obscurantism. The Christian Church has had a bad record on this debate. One part of the Christian Church in America was so apologetic about the faith of revelation in history, that it sold out its faith to modern culture, saying, "We do not mean anything more than what the sociologists mean." Another part of the church was so anxious to guard the Christian faith in its uniqueness that it was betrayed into obscurantism. Modern fundamentalism has a frantic way of hiding its treasure in a napkin in order that it might be presented to the Lord undefiled. We must avoid these two perils.

Our task then is to guard and to expound the uniqueness and vitality of the Christian faith. We recall what Pascal called the misery and dignity of man, and we should try to relate that double dimension to our teaching and preaching. Pascal defied the rationalism of his day. The philosophers, he said, "can tell me about man's dignity, and they drive me to pride, or about man's misery, and they drive me to despair. Where, but in the simplicity of the gospel will I know about both the dignity and the misery of man?"

These words were spoken in the seventeenth century. They are relevant to our task today.

Notes and Sources

Passages quoted in the Introduction are from the following sources, listed in the order they are first used: INTERVIEW: Arthur Herzog, "A Visit with Reinhold Niebuhr," *Think,* December 1959. ADDRESS: on theological education, to entering students at Union Theological Seminary, September 25, 1955. BOOK: *Leaves From the Notebook of a Tamed Cynic,* 1929. ARTICLE: "Worship and the Social Conscience," *Radical Religion,* Winter 1937; reprinted in *Essays in Applied Christianity,* edited by D. B. Robertson, 1959. ARTICLE: "Some Things I Have Learned," in *What I Have Learned,* edited by Saturday Review Editors, 1958. ARTICLE: "The Problem of the Modern Church: Triviality," *Christianity and Crisis,* August 4, 1969. ADDRESS: "The Hazards and Difficulties of the Christian Ministry," a speech for the Conference on the Ministry, Union Theological Seminary, March 29, 1953. INTERVIEW: Patrick Granfield, "An Interview with Reinhold Niebuhr," in *Theologians at Work,* 1968.

Index of Themes of the Prayers

Brotherhood   46, 47, 48, 49, 72, 73, 96

Christian Ministry   47, 49, 73, 112, 113–14, 115, 116, 118

Faith   113, 122–24

God the Creator   23, 24, 26, 27, 46, 47, 49, 103, 112, 113, 114, 119

Grace   46, 48, 96, 101, 102, 104, 112, 113, 115, 116

Humility and Contrition   12, 24, 27, 28, 70, 71, 102, 103, 104, 117, 120–22

Joy in Creation   23, 24, 46–47, 103

Judgment and Redemption   26, 28, 47, 97, 98, 99, 100–101, 114

Peace   73–74, 75, 98, 99–100, 101, 102, 116–17

Power and Mercy of God   26, 27, 75, 97–98, 99, 100, 102–3, 104, 115, 117, 118

Responsibilities of Mankind   12, 49–50, 70, 72–73, 96–98, 117–18

Sacramental Occasions   124–25, 125–26, 126–27

Social Justice   24, 25, 48–50, 70–72, 96–104

Sufferings of Mankind   48, 70, 71, 72, 73, 74, 75, 101